"Although racism impacts us profoundly, it remains a sensitive and polarizing topic that is difficult to broach in many faith communities. Conor Kelly provides an opening. Drawing from the traditional frameworks and resources of Catholic moral theology, he supplies an introduction to the social dimensions of racism. *Racism and Structural Sin* is both nuanced and accessible, useful for faith formation as well the seminary, undergraduate, and high school classroom."

—Joseph S. Flipper, Mary Ann Spearin Chair of Catholic Theology, University of Dayton

Racism
and Structural Sin

*Confronting Injustice
with the Eyes of Faith*

Conor M. Kelly

Foreword by Carolyn Y. Woo

LITURGICAL PRESS
Collegeville, Minnesota

www.litpress.org

Cover design by John Vineyard. Art courtesy of Getty Images.

Some of this work originally appeared in Conor Kelly, "Systemic Racism as Cultural and Structural Sin: Distinctive Contributions from Catholic Social Thought," *Journal of Catholic Social Thought* 20, no. 1 (Winter 2023).

1   2   3   4   5   6   7   8   9

Library of Congress Cataloging-in-Publication Data

Names: Kelly, Conor M., author.
Title: Racism and structural sin : confronting injustice with the eyes of faith / Conor M. Kelly.
Description: Collegeville, Minnesota : Liturgical Press, 2023. | Includes bibliographical references. | Summary: "As a people of faith inspired by the belief that every human person is created in the image and likeness of God, Catholics have a responsibility to be champions for racial justice. Racism and Structural Sin invites readers to confront racism not only on a personal level but also the root causes and perpetuated structures of this sin. Grounded in church teaching and pastoral practice, this book is a resource for Catholics-especially White Catholics-looking to wrestle with the challenges of race in the United States today through the eyes of their faith"— Provided by publisher.
Identifiers: LCCN 2022043037 (print) | LCCN 2022043038 (ebook) | ISBN 9780814667835 (trade paperback) | ISBN 9780814667842 (epub) | ISBN 9780814667842 (pdf) | ISBN 9780814669358 (pdf)
Subjects: LCSH: Race relations—Catholic Church. | Racism—Religious aspects— Catholic Church. | BISAC: RELIGION / Christian Theology / Ethics | RELIGION / Christian Living / Social Issues
Classification: LCC BX1795.R33 K43 2023 (print) | LCC BX1795.R33 (ebook) | DDC 282/.73089—dc23/eng20230207
LC record available at https://lccn.loc.gov/2022043037
LC ebook record available at https://lccn.loc.gov/2022043038

Contents

Foreword

This book by Conor Kelly serves all Christians by calling us to see the realities of racism, acknowledge our roles in both our personal behavior and its cumulative effect on existing structures, contrast this with the teachings of God, and seek conversion relying on God's grace and the power of the Holy Spirit.

When our granddaughter was born, with utmost attention we studied her features looking for any traits of her quarter-Chinese heritage. With strawberry fuzz (hair), blue eyes, and the fairest complexion, Sammie at this point shows no indications of her Oriental parentage.

My first emotion: relief.

It caught me by surprise. After all, I have managed to prosper in America as a Chinese immigrant. I have pushed deep down all the jokes, assumptions, and taunts directed at me as a person of Asian descent. There were "Chinese whore" jokes from the sweetest young woman who wanted to draw me in and who eventually became a minister; an assignment by an academic counselor to a remedial English class without any testing—her intention was to help me succeed; a retort from a classmate whom I was tutoring in math when he told me the best help I could give him was to withdraw and not blow the curve in the class.

I remember the heartbreak and fury when my son was taunted as a "China-man" when he started his first day in kindergarten. The hapless student intern managed the only apologetic response she could muster by throwing up her hands. Come to think of it, it was the first time I allowed myself to feel fury, not just resigned acceptance: the price to pay for being an outsider. A neighbor was intentionally knocked down to the ground by a teenage boy on a bike screaming at her to go back to her own country: she is US-born Japanese American. There are good friends of mine, supporters of racial justice, who would make jokes of a non-native speaker's English and others who would laugh at it. They attribute the other's discomfort to "over-sensitivity."

Lately, each story I hear of random slurs and violent acts against different groups have raised my wariness that we are indeed targeted, even while being celebrated, for our skin color, religion, sexual identity, etc. I feel acutely the pernicious infection of racism in our country.

At the same time, I know my success also derives from a system that favors merit with little attention to the accessibility to factors that make success more likely in the first place. Recently, an acquaintance lost her son to gun violence. Our zip codes differ by one digit at the end: we are essentially neighbors. Yet our worlds might as well be separated by unpassable rivers, canyons, and mountains far beyond the other side of Main Street. Our children face vastly different probabilities of being shot; enjoy vastly different educational resources; navigate vastly different daily challenges; and imbibe vastly different visions of what is possible and within reach.

This book takes on the personal behavior and social structures that perpetuate racism in our society. Kelly correctly points out that many people do not embrace ill or explicit intent to act as a "racist." They would find such behavior repugnant. At the same time, referencing St. Thomas Aquinas, good intentions do not always yield good outcomes. He calls us to recognize our narrow and partial understanding of the other, and the influences of our environment in shaping our judgments. Kelly is not after indictments, but humility and awareness of our own limitations.

Centuries of personal attitudes, biases, and the pursuit of self-interests of those in power shape policies, regulations, practices, and enforcements that comprise the structure of our society.

The structures are as real physically as the walls, hallways, and doorways that block or enable access within spaces. Embedded in social and political structures, these elements govern the ease and pathways by which different groups, delineated by economic, ethnic, and racial markers, find their ways to education, housing, healthcare, and professions.

As Kelly writes, the desire for safe neighborhoods, quality education for our children, or resources that enable flourishing are genuine goods. It is right to want them. Structural sin emerges when such endowments are systematically blocked for other groups, when we derive advantages at others' expense, or when we keep silent, condone, and actually lock in such asymmetries.

Kelly accesses our Christian faith through the teachings of scriptures and the magisterium to label both personal and structural racism as offenses against God. God created all people in his image and thus imbued them with sacredness. Human dignity is imparted by God as his personal handprint on each person. As Kelly rightly notes, to be complicit in systems that diminish others' dignity and subordinate their well-being for our own comfort is a form of spiritual sickness.

The way back is conversion: an about-face turn of our eyes and our hearts toward God. Kelly urges us to pursue a genuine faith that trusts in the power of the Holy Spirit and commit to fervent prayer. We are to act on this conversion: advocate for and contribute to the education, healthcare, and safety for other groups that we want for own children; or raise our voice and objection when these are missing for lower income, migrant, or minority segments. On a personal level, to not let a joke casually overlook the dignity of the person bearing the brunt of the joke; and to accept that consideration of the impact on others is a responsibility beyond benign intent. Racism is an ugly and wicked problem: it is perpetuated by ignorance, fear, and self-interest. Even so, it is no match for God's grace, which is available to us for the asking.

I am committed and energized to teach Sammie about her Chinese heritage: the incredibly beautiful traditions, devotion to family, rich culture, history, and innovations as well as her challenges, suffering, and mistakes. I also embrace the responsibility to teach her how to engage a society that pegs her as "the other." However, I felt something was missing until I finished this book. The first lesson is not the magnificence of China, but the magnificence of God who made all people to be like him, to be glorious, and to be love for each other.

Carolyn Y. Woo, PhD

Introduction

For much of my life, I thought I was in a good place with respect to the challenges of racism. I never witnessed overt forms of racial bigotry among anyone I knew growing up, so I assumed my social circle was accepting and understanding. My parents instilled in me and my older brother a deeply Catholic respect for the innate dignity of every human person, leaving little room for racist tropes about the "inferiority" of some and the "superiority" of others to take hold. And in school, I learned about the injustices of legalized racial segregation and came to lionize the leaders of the civil rights movement as true American heroes who paved the way for a more just and equitable society. In short, I was taught to cultivate what (White) people typically describe as "enlightened" attitudes about race and racism: we are all equal, there should be no discrimination based on the color of one's skin, and there is no reason to harbor animosity toward those who might look different from us. As a result of these experiences and convictions, I felt I could happily—and credibly—claim that racism, with the possible exception of the isolated attitudes and actions of a few bad apples, was mainly a thing of the past in U.S. society.

During my college years, however, my confidence in the adequacy of these convictions began to waiver. My college campus, while still predominantly White, was more diverse than the community where I grew up. I assumed my enlightened attitudes would allow me to make new connections across racial lines, but my peer group was not instantly diverse. An attitude of openness and acceptance, I realized, may be necessary in a diverse society, but it is hardly sufficient for building meaningful relationships. There were larger structural factors that left many students of color, especially Black students, uncomfortable on campus. Individual attitudes could only go so far.

Helpfully, I did have substantive conversations, both inside and outside the classroom, with my classmates from all racial backgrounds about race and racism in the United States. More than anything, these discussions taught me that I did not have the complete picture I once thought I had. My experience of a childhood free from racial bigotry may have been genuine, but it was just that: my experience. Not all my classmates could say the same. In fact, many of them—again, especially my Black classmates— had experienced bigotry and discrimination directly. I therefore lost my confidence that racism was a thing of the past. Even more importantly, I slowly began to appreciate that a comprehensive awareness of life in the United States could not emerge from the narrow slice of my own experience alone but instead required insights from others whose respective experiences with this country and its long, varied history could fill in the gaps I did not even see. As a result, I arrived at a place where I finally recognized that diverse relationships were not a nice benefit for those who wanted them but a true necessity for anyone who wanted to affirm the sacredness of every human life and whose faith calls them to foster an "authentic culture of encounter," to borrow one of Pope Francis's favorite phrases.[1]

Flash forward about a dozen years, though, and we get to the point where my personal story becomes much more embarrassing. I can talk a good game about my intellectual journey to an appreciation of diversity, but then I must also admit that I do not have much to show for it in practical terms. More than a decade after my collegiate epiphanies, my social circle is *less* racially diverse. I have since planted roots in what is, by some measures, the most segregated metropolitan area in the United States, but I am not leading the charge for happily integrated neighborhoods.

I have instead ensconced myself and my family in a rich suburb with good schools, beautiful green spaces, and overwhelmingly White neighbors. I am—not to put too fine a point on it—part of the very problem I thought I had begun to overcome with my cognitive transformations.

How do I reconcile this reality with my convictions, including my Catholic faith? The short answer is that I do not, or at least not completely. I live with an uneasy tension, and, quite frankly, I struggle with it.

Sometimes, the struggle fades into the background, like when my wife and I recognized that the call to care for our extended family made this community the obvious place to stay long-term. Other times, the struggle bursts into the foreground. I remember a student's heartfelt question after a class discussion on racial segregation in Milwaukee in which she indicated she had no idea how she could find a morally "good" place to live if she stayed in the area after graduation. That generated a lot of soul-searching. Then, of course, as a national racial reckoning took hold in summer 2020 in response to the brutal police killing of George Floyd, I could hardly pretend the tensions in my own life had been resolved. Instead, I had to once again confront my own complicities in racism and its legacies in the United States, and I cannot claim my conscience was especially relieved by the results.

I say all this here because I want to be clear that I am not writing this book about racism based on the assumption that I have all the answers. I am writing this book precisely because I am still trying to figure out what those answers should be. On matters of race and racism, I resonate much less with the image of a perfect anti-racist who has broken free from the constraints of a flawed society and much more with the humble self-description of Pope Francis, who famously answered a question about his true identity by claiming, "I am a sinner whom the Lord has looked upon."[2] This book, therefore, is not an attempt to condemn others for their failure to reach the rarefied illumination I enjoy. It should be quite clear from my own brief admissions that I do not occupy the perch that would be necessary to lob such accusations. Instead, this book is built around the efforts I have taken—and continue to take—to remove the "wooden beam" (Matt 7:3-5) from my eye so that I can live a more faith-filled life in a country riven by racial injustices.

A part of my ongoing struggle, this book is meant to be a resource for other Catholics who are similarly interested in wrestling with the challenges of race in the United States today using the eyes of our faith. If the past few years have taught us anything, it is that we should all be invested in this task, but I continue to see that we, as a church, have not yet responded to this call. In parish after parish, we seem more reluctant than ever to have an honest conversation about race and racism. Part of the problem is that we are not sure how to have such a frank discussion. The other part is that we know this process will force us to confront our own failures, and we would rather avoid that uncomfortable evaluation.

This book is designed to address both of these challenges. First, it uses the resources of our shared faith to give ordinary Catholics a clearer entryway into the ongoing national conversation about racism in the United States. By offering an expressly theological account of the current racial injustices fracturing our nation, the book connects larger ideas like structural racism to Catholic concepts like structural sin, making it easier to see that our faith does call us to action in this pivotal moment. In this way, the book builds on my expertise not so much as an anti-racist (although I am certainly working on being one) but as a Catholic moral theologian, for although I admitted that I do not have all the answers on these matters, the thing I have not yet acknowledged is that I am in a unique position to know where to look for them. Between a Ph.D. in theological ethics and an active teaching and research agenda that includes writing about the implications of Catholic social teaching for everyday life, I am intimately familiar with the tools our faith provides for the difficult conversations we need to have. I ask, therefore, that readers not dismiss me for my limitations but instead assess the significance of the theological claims found throughout this book on their own terms. I am not appealing to my own life as an exemplary illustration of how to live; I am appealing to our common faith tradition to highlight the ends for which all Catholics—myself very much included—should strive.

Second, because the book is grounded in my own efforts to wrestle with the legacies of racism in my life, it also responds to the hesitancy many U.S. Catholics have about tackling an uncomfortable topic that is directly tied to our past shortcomings. I hope that my honesty about my own moral failures in this area can lay the groundwork for others to explore what our faith tells us about confronting racism without feeling threatened by the fear of what that examination might reveal about themselves. Here, I am thinking most especially of my fellow White Catholics. Our Black Catholic brothers and sisters stress that we are the people who need to have a faith-inspired conversation about racism the most, but we are simultaneously the ones who are the least inclined to do so.[3] At the heart of this tension is something that public discourse often refers to as "white fragility," which essentially describes the tendency of many White people to avoid conversations about race and racism at all costs because these discussions often make them feel bad.[4] If we are going to make any progress as a church and as a nation, White people like myself need to overcome this initial reaction. Helpfully, I believe that my own experience and my expertise can combine to chip away at some of this reflexive resistance. Let me offer one quick illustration.

Precisely because I have been struggling as a theologian to interrogate the ways I continue to contribute to larger racial injustices like residential segregation, not just as a theoretical question but as a very real practical matter, I have a personal grasp of the complicated factors shaping the status quo on race relations in the United States. I know, for example, that my contributions to this problem did not emerge from a malicious set of discriminatory beliefs but rather resulted from an effort to pursue genuine goods. I wanted good schools for my children, walking paths for my family's health and safety, a sense of community that left everyone feeling valued, and security for us and our neighbors. These are not ill-formed desires; they are precisely the kinds of goods that the Catholic tradition recognizes as essential to human flourishing. They are, in other words, the same goods that any human person would want—and, in fact, *should* want—for themselves and their families. Theologically, I would identify these goods as an essential part of the "common good," which the Second Vatican Council's *Gaudium et Spes* describes as "the sum total of social conditions which allow people, either as groups or as individuals, to reach their fulfillment more fully and more easily" (no. 26).[5]

The trouble, of course, is that our society is not yet built to ensure that these common goods are equally available to all social groups and their individual members. On the contrary, in areas of the country marred by racial segregation (a description that sadly captures most areas of the country, at least according to current census data), these goods are not just unevenly distributed; they are unjustly clustered by race. By pursuing these genuine goods in such a context and prioritizing them without any real thought to the larger forces involved, I pushed myself and my family toward the Whiter areas of our metropolitan region, ultimately reinforcing a situation that I would swear I never wanted to exist let alone persist.

My training as a moral theologian points to an obvious explanation for this result, for the Catholic moral tradition reminds us that the best of intentions are not sufficient to yield the best moral outcomes. Indeed, good, albeit mistaken, intentions are often at the heart of our worst moral choices. As St. Thomas Aquinas (1225–74) explained in his famous treatise on Catholic doctrine, his *Summa Theologiae*, human beings who are made in the image and likeness of God never turn toward evil for its own sake. Instead, we always seek to achieve some good, and we can therefore trace all our sins back to a fundamental misperception: we chose a bad end under the guise of a good; what we thought was in our best interest actually undercut our human nature.[6] In many ways, my housing choices were a simple manifestation of this classic mix-up. I saw good things that I wanted for my family, but I focused on a partial good alone. I got good schools, but I also became yet another data point enshrining racial segregation in Milwaukee.

Significantly, this traditional perspective from Catholic moral theology offers two insights that can preclude a reactionary retreat into White resistance when matters of racism arise. First, Aquinas's account of how White people like me go astray shows that there is no reason to indict people's motivations or even doubt their good intentions. His moral vision insists that it is not only possible but also highly likely for someone to contribute to a bad outcome without consciously seeking evil. In fact, such a disconnect between good intentions and bad results is, in this quintessential framework of our faith, the expected explanation for most of our worst actions as human beings. Thus, to put this first insight into more personal terms, Aquinas's analysis allows me to admit that I am part of the problem of racial segregation without suggesting that I intended to perpetuate the injustices that I know I loathe.

For any White Catholics who find themselves in similar circumstances, this interpretation should be disarming, hopefully to the point that it can provide an opening for a more serious assessment of racism in the United States and our relationship with it. Nevertheless, this analysis does not get anyone off the hook, for as much as this explanation can leave one's motives intact, it simultaneously underscores, in its second insight, that a form of evil has occurred. Furthermore, it directly challenges any attempt to ignore responsibility, because this explanation also insists that the evil transpired because of failures on our part. Aquinas's interpretation may grant that we were seeking a good end, but it also asserts that we missed the mark, largely because our priorities were corrupted. We pretended we were seeking what we should have been, but because we were operating with an incomplete view of what it means to "have life and have it more abundantly" (John 10:10), we continue to suffer the effects of sin and evil in our world.

To shift this sinful state of affairs, we need to better understand the ways we have managed to undermine that common good, both in what we have done *and in what we have failed to do* (to draw from the *Confiteor* we say at Mass). Specifically, we need to take an explicit look at race and racism and examine the moments in which we, as Catholics, have ceased to be a people who "thinks in terms of community and the priority of the life of all over the appropriation of goods by a few" (*Evangelii Gaudium*, no. 188)[7] and have instead become consumed as individuals—and especially, for those to whom it applies, as White individuals—with the goal of securing goods for ourselves at the expense of others. We need to get to a place where we can attend to the crucial point that Aquinas, and the broader Catholic moral tradition, reveals so emphatically: good intentions are not enough to bring about the goodness of our flourishing as human beings, let alone the goodness of our flourishing at a societal level.

We need, in other words, to look beyond personal choices to see the broader, structural features shaping our world because the hard truth is that those structures are dictating the effects of our choices, generating racial injustices that few of us would ever accept if we had to select them directly for ourselves. To make sense of this reality, we need to take a long hard look at the systemic features that make it easier for us to choose narrow forms of self-interest rather than prioritize the life of all. We need to have a conversation about structural racism through the eyes of our faith.

Through four parts, each containing two short chapters, this book provides resources for this essential conversation so that we can emerge with a more critical account of what it takes to pursue the common good in a society whose structures remain very much haunted by the legacies of slavery, Jim Crow, outright bigotry, and numerous other forms of racial exclusion. The first part examines the Catholic obligation to confront racism in all its forms, demonstrating that an attentiveness to racism's personal *and social* dimensions is very much a presupposition of the Catholic challenge to this persistent sin. The second part explains how the concept of structural sin found in Catholic social teaching can help us make sense of racism's structural manifestations so that Catholics, who are informed by Aquinas's awareness of the potential gap between intentions and results, can recognize how racism persists even when a community's shared intentions are not aiming at this end. The third part applies these categories to interpret the current state of four shared social institutions—policing, housing, healthcare, and education—revealing ways racism functions as a structural sin in the United States today. Finally, the fourth part explores strategies for confronting this structural sin using insights from what the *Compendium of the Social Doctrine of the Church* describes as the four "permanent principles of Catholic social doctrine" (no. 160).[8] The result is a new set of tools for a distinctly Catholic contribution to the conversation about racial justice that we desperately need to pursue as a country and as a church. It is, in this sense, another chapter in my struggle and, hopefully, a new step in our journey of faith.

Questions for Reflection and Discussion

1. To what extent do you resist conversations about race and racism? What in your experiences has contributed to this hesitancy or lack thereof?

2. How do you react to Aquinas's assertion that sin arises from our pursuit of genuine goods to the wrong extent or in the wrong manner, rather than from a desire for an evil outcome on its own? Does the application of this account to racial segregation resonate with you or frustrate you? Why?

3. As you review the brief outline of this book's four parts in the last paragraph of the chapter, which parts are you most interested in exploring? Which are you most apprehensive about?

PART I

The Catholic Obligation to Confront Racism

As noted in the introduction, the point of this first part is to articulate the ways our Catholic faith demands a rejection and active confrontation of racism in all its forms. Chapters 1 and 2 demonstrate this point by discussing two distinct manifestations of racism, one personal and one social, to lay the foundation for what a comprehensive response to racism will look like. Although these categories are increasingly common in our public discourse, especially as conversations shift to include notions like systemic racism, the emphasis in these next two chapters is intentionally theological. At times, I will talk about the ways personal and social forms of racism are described in our broader public discourse in order to further explain the categories, but the fundamental claim in part I is that these conventional categories align with the Catholic condemnation of racism as a sin and are valuable for that reason.

CHAPTER ONE

Personal Manifestations of Racism

On June 3, 2020, just over a week after a Minneapolis police officer's physical restraint killed George Floyd and sparked nationwide protests, Pope Francis concluded his regularly scheduled weekly audience with a poignant appeal to his "dear brothers and sisters in the United States." Acknowledging the "tragic death of Mr. George Floyd" and the ensuing "social unrest," the pope insisted, "We cannot tolerate or turn a blind eye to racism and exclusion in any form and yet claim to defend the sacredness of every human life."[1]

Pope Francis's words situate racism as a theological challenge and helpfully illustrate why Catholics have an acute obligation to confront racism. Our faith calls us to recognize and honor the inherent dignity of every human person, for we believe each human being is made in the image and likeness of God. Racism denies that dignity and contradicts our commitment to uphold the sanctity of life. As the U.S. Catholic bishops explained in their most recent pastoral letter against racism, *Open Wide Our Hearts*, "The injustice and harm racism causes are an attack on human life." Racism is, as they go on to explain, "a life issue" (30).[2]

How, then, do we honor our commitments to the sanctity of life in a world where "instances of racism continue to shame us

. . . show[ing] that our supposed social progress is not as real or definitive as we think" (*Fratelli Tutti*, no. 20)?[3] On one level, the answer is simple. To borrow Pope Francis's language, we refuse to turn a blind eye to racism and exclusion in any form. On another level, however, the answer is much more complicated, for racism and exclusion come in many forms. This fact means that an effective Catholic response to racism, one that honors our recognition of racism as a life issue in a church that is committed to the protection and promotion of the intrinsic value of every human life, must be multifaceted. We must appreciate that racism is a sinful phenomenon that operates on more than one plane, and we must develop distinct responses for each of these manifestations.

The point of this chapter is to address the personal plane, where Catholic theology helps us recognize that an effective stand against racism needs to begin within. To explain this responsibility, the chapter discusses what racism means at a personal level and provides a theological explanation for the fact that racism continues to haunt our society on this personal plane. This yields a clearer sense of the kind of response to personal racism that our Catholic faith demands and lays a foundation for the next chapter, which provides a similar analysis of racism on the social plane.

An Intuitive Account of Racism

At the personal level, we can define racism according to what Bryan Massingale, a Black Catholic priest, moral theologian, and leading expert on the theological dimensions of racism in the United States, calls the "commonsense understanding" of racism. In this definition, "Person A (usually, but not always, white) consciously, deliberately, and intentionally does something negative to person B (usually, but not always, black or Latino) because of the color of his or her skin."[4] As Massingale notes, this account pinpoints racism in the *intentional* actions of *personal* agents that have a *negative, discriminatory* effect on others *based on* their racial identity.

For reasons that will be discussed in further detail in the next chapter, this definition of racism is not sufficient on its own to support a robust Catholic contribution to the ongoing racial reckoning in the United States. Nevertheless, it offers a detailed way of appreciating how racism functions on the personal plane, and so the commonsense definition provides an appropriate starting point for a theological analysis of racism. In fact, simply reflecting on the commonsense definition yields two valuable insights.

First, the reason Massingale calls this intentional, interpersonal description of racism the commonsense definition is that it is the understanding that is most readily denounced. Virtually all observers would agree with labeling an action that meets the above criteria as racist, and the condemnation of such behavior would be swift and strict. Thus, although it technically remains legal for private clubs in the United States to discriminate on the basis of race—say, by admitting only White members—few people would agree with the argument that this practice is entirely acceptable simply because it is not illegal. Instead, most would bristle at the idea that potential members are excluded strictly due their racial background and would castigate the practice.

This instinct to reject displays of commonsense racism is a good and commendable one that reflects one way in which our collective conscience is at least attuned to the right values. Not too long ago, we would have had trouble asserting that the commonsense definition of racism was truly a matter of common sense in the United States. There was a time, for instance, when parents actively encouraged their children to commit conscious, deliberate, and intentional acts of vilification and hate against other human beings because of the color of their skin. How else can one explain the hostile crowds seeking to prevent the "Little Rock Nine," the brave group of nine Black students who were the first to integrate Little Rock's Central High School in the aftermath of *Brown v. Board of Education*, from entering their new school in 1957? That kind of animosity, which we would now decry as commonsense racism, only flourished then because the social context allowed it to do so.

Today, thankfully, we are in a different place. The moral unacceptability of commonsense racism is, indeed, a commonsense judgment. Hence, when the U.S. Catholic bishops insisted in *Open Wide Our Hearts* that "racist acts are sinful because they violate justice" and added, "They reveal a failure to acknowledge the human dignity of the persons offended, to recognize them as the neighbors Christ calls us to love (Mt 22:39)," few readers objected to the claim (3). Instead, Catholics and non-Catholics alike affirmed the idea that manifestations of commonsense racism are violations of justice that must be challenged.

This first insight thus gives us some cause for consolation, as it suggests the growth and development of our collective conscience as a nation. Any comfort must be quickly tempered by a second insight, though, which is that a gap remains between theory and practice even in the sphere of commonsense racism. While we can quickly, and gratefully, assert that the moral flaws of commonsense racism are no longer subject to denial or debate, we cannot realistically claim that we have consistently overcome even this most overt form of racism. Racist slurs routinely mar sporting matches, and the number of occurrences of racial harassment on social media—including reports of high school students who started a "Slave Trade" group for "auctioning off Black classmates" in Oregon[5]—are depressingly frequent. We may have a commonsense language for condemning certain actions, but the actions themselves have not gone away. On the contrary, they continue among people who would adamantly insist they are not racist and who would be regarded as "normal" by their peers in virtually every other way.

Racism, even the commonsense racism of the personal plane, remains "one particularly destructive *and persistent* form of evil . . . [that] still infects our nation" (*Open Wide Our Hearts*, 3, emphasis added). As a result, there is a practical disconnect between the abstract rejection of commonsense racism that we believe to be widely shared and the persistence of racist actions, even the most widely rejected commonsense ones, throughout our public life. To get a sense of how we might account for this gap, we need to turn to the Sermon on the Mount.

An Interior Examination

One of my favorite things about the Sermon on the Mount, at least in Matthew's presentation of it (chaps. 5–7), is the way Jesus leaves the crowds "astonished at his teaching" (7:28). For those who are familiar with the Sermon on the Mount, this might seem a bit surprising because "Blessed are the merciful" (5:7) sounds fairly straightforward the eightieth time you hear it. If we try to imagine what it would have been like to experience the sermon for the first time, however, I think it becomes easier to see the astonishing nature of Jesus's teachings.

When I reread Matthew 5–7 in an attempt to hear the text anew, the element that stands out most to me is not the Beatitudes or the sayings on prayer and fasting but the "antitheses," a series of powerful contrasts in 5:21-48 meant to highlight how God's demands are more encompassing than the standards humans prefer to set for themselves, even when those standards are based on traditional laws from the Torah. Perhaps because I am an ethicist, I am always drawn to the moral one-upmanship involved in these proclamations. You have heard it said that you shouldn't take more than a single eye for an eye or a tooth for a tooth? Well, I say don't even take the tooth! Instead, turn the other cheek and let them smack you upside the head—twice!

Read without any added context, these sayings truly are remarkable. Once I get past the shock, however, I can usually see the call to a deeper kind of moral commitment. As the Jesuit Scripture scholar Daniel Harrington explained, often the antitheses in the Sermon on the Mount are not direct contrasts but rather an invitation to see the original law in a new way, allowing Jesus to "extend the commandment's scope by going to the root of the abuse."[6] Instead of simply condemning adultery, for instance, Jesus calls for the rejection of lust; instead of a painless (for most of us, I hope) forsaking of murder, Jesus demands the more comprehensive abandonment of anger.

With these teachings, Jesus reminds us that refraining from objectionable practices will only get us so far in our efforts to lead good moral lives. If we genuinely want to answer the call, then we must not only avoid bad behaviors but also work to remove the problematic attitudes and desires that lurk within us and make the wrong actions seem appealing in the first place. Essentially, Jesus says that without tackling these internal shortcomings, we might temporarily shift our behaviors, but we will not actually transform our way of life. Simply put, there will always be a malformed set of assumptions lurking within us, just waiting to pop up.

This central assertion of the antitheses is crucial for understanding the obstacles we still face in confronting racism today. While we have widely sought to remove racist actions from the public life we share together, we have not yet given sufficient attention to the assumptions and attitudes that lurk within us on both a personal and social level. The main reason we can simultaneously say that our society condemns the personal manifestations of commonsense racism and that these personal manifestations still exist in our society is that we face the very problem that Jesus underscores in the Sermon on the Mount: external actions have internal roots, and it is much harder to change the latter than the former.

The close relationship between internal attitudes and external actions has special relevance for the fight against racism. As the U.S. Catholic bishops stress, "Racism can often be found in our hearts—in many cases placed there unwillingly or unknowingly by our upbringing and culture. As such, it can lead to thoughts and actions that we do not even see as racist, but nonetheless flow from the same prejudicial root" (*Open Wide Our Hearts*, 5). At this interior level, racism can be stubbornly tenacious because it has the ability to capitalize on natural human tendencies to categorize "in-groups" and "out-groups." According to psychologists, this instinct lingers to this day because it had evolutionary advantages for our ancestors, allowing them to separate members of their immediate kin group, whom they knew they could trust, from the strangers whose trustworthiness was still uncertain.[7] Because this simplistic separation allowed our predecessors to survive in a violent world, our brains have become trained to recognize differences more readily than similarities.

This ingrained predisposition is not inherently a bad thing. If we would simply recognize differences and then find a way to value them, we could even use this capacity to our advantage. The problem is that we rarely subject our instincts to this degree of critical scrutiny. Instead, we typically see differences and stop there, using distinctions much as our ancestors did: to delineate a group we would identify as "us" from everyone else, who is simply defined as "them." However much this strategy may have served a biological function, it contrasts sharply with Jesus's insistence that his followers have an obligation to love all their neighbors, not just the ones who look like them. As can be seen in the parable of the Good Samaritan and Jesus's frequent shocking statements relativizing familial obligations—see Matthew 12:46-50, for instance, where Jesus pretends not to know his own mother in order to make a point about following God's will—Jesus made the rejection of the conventional identity categories that would otherwise constrain our love of neighbor a central feature of his preaching. The juxtaposition with our evolutionary instincts could hardly be starker, for, in the bishops' own words, "when we start to see some people as 'them' and others as 'us,' we fail to love" (*Open Wide Our Hearts*, 17).

One of our essential responsibilities in confronting racism, then, is to become more aware of our internal attitudes and presuppositions. Precisely because we are hardwired to attend to differences, we must consciously examine our reactions to the differences that we see. If we do not do this intentionally, racist perspectives from the world around us will infect our evaluations of difference unconsciously because it is easier for racist prejudices to get into our heads than it is for us to remove them from our hearts.

Sociologists describe these unconsciously accepted attitudes as forms of "implicit bias," a type of prejudicial interpretation of differences that we accept from our cultural surroundings un-critically and that becomes our default mode of interpreting our interactions across racial groups. In more theological terms, the U.S. Catholic bishops have decried instances in which "racial bias affects our personal attitudes and judgments," arguing that when "we allow another's race to influence our relationship and limit our openness . . . [we] see yet close our hearts to our brothers and sisters in need" (*Brothers and Sisters to Us*).[8] Fr. Massingale, meanwhile, simply argues that "at its deepest level, racism is a soul sickness" because of the way it perverts our instincts.[9]

What all these analyses reveal is the age-old connection between our inner selves and our outer actions that informed Jesus's six antitheses in the Sermon on the Mount. This link, and racism's tragic exploitation of it, means that the only productive way to challenge racism is to begin by prioritizing conversion.

Conversion is, most fundamentally, an internal process of repri-oritization. The Greek term for conversion found in the gospels, *metanoia*, denotes a physical turning around that has a person choosing to change course in a way that simultaneously entails moving *away from* the direction they had been going and *toward* a new destination. For the personal plane of commonsense racism, this kind of conversion means intentionally deciding to let go of the prejudicial assumptions our culture tends to attach to different racial groups and move toward a more positive vision of those our brains prime us to instinctively categorize as "other."

In a popular TED Talk on responding to biases, Netflix execu-tive and author Vernā Myers puts a literal spin on this process. Noting how many unarmed Black men have been the victims of the excessive use of police force, Myers describes a cultural association between Black male bodies and a sense of threat to personal safety and argues that one way to counteract these biases is to move toward young Black men rather than away from them in personal encounters.[10] Her strategy captures *metanoia* in a truly incarnational way, encouraging us to use our bodies to interrogate our internal presuppositions. It is a valuable tool for encouraging the kind of conscious decision-making that we must employ if we are going to break free from the stereotyping that allows commonsense racism to simmer below the surface on a personal level.

Even with this literal form of *metanoia*, though, we must not forget that the end goal is an interior transformation, and this is not a process we are supposed to undertake on our own. The *metanoia* that allows us to turn away from sin toward the path of discipleship is a grace-filled process that comes not from our sheer will but from the working of the Holy Spirit in our lives. An essential part of the pursuit of conversion, then, must be a prayerful openness to God's intervention in our hearts. As Fr. Massingale stresses in his identification of racism as a spiritual problem, "this soul sickness can only be healed by deep prayer . . . [because] only an invasion of divine love will shatter the small images of God that enable us to live undisturbed by the racism that benefits some and terrorizes so many."[11]

Finally, while conversion is properly an interior change, it is always actualized in external behaviors. Just as "faith without works is dead" (Jas 2:26), so a conversion that has no material implications is stalled. Consequently, we must not think solely about ways to challenge problematic internal attitudes regarding racial difference; we must also find the means to enact our new commitments in our interactions with others.

The U.S. Catholic bishops have some practical suggestions for this process. In *Brothers and Sisters to Us*, their 1979 pastoral letter on racism, the bishops articulate specific actions that should flow from the *metanoia* they countenance. Specifically, they point to "rejecting racial stereotypes, racial slurs and racial jokes" as an external illustration of the internal change that conversion entails, and they encourage "a personal commitment to join with others in political efforts to bring about justice for the victims" of racism. Recalling Jesus's insistence that "[b]y their fruits you will know them" (Matt 7:16), we must find ways to walk the walk and not just talk the talk when we strive to turn away from racism's roots within us.

Conclusion

The best way to think about the Catholic obligation to confront racism at the personal level is to think about conversion as the fundamental call of the Gospel. When we embrace the message of the antitheses in the Sermon on the Mount and acknowledge that a permanent removal of sinful actions requires a deeper rejection of problematic attitudes, we can appreciate that a careful evaluation of our own presuppositions about the people who do not look exactly like us is essential if we are going to accept that racism is a life issue. Indeed, with this perspective, we can recognize that a prayerful examination of our own consciences and an honest petition to God to open wide our hearts are absolute prerequisites for anyone who accepts that commonsense racism needs to be removed from our world not just in theory but also in practice.

Notably, while this individual process of personal conversion is indispensable—given the theological assumptions found in the Sermon on the Mount—it will not be enough on its own. As the next chapter will make clear, a proper Catholic response to racism needs to attend to the social plane as well as the personal one.

Questions for Reflection and Discussion

1. What is your reaction to the U.S. Catholic bishops' categorization of racism as a life issue? What do you think they mean by this, and what does this say about the importance of responding to racism for Catholics?

2. To what extent do you agree that Massingale's "commonsense understanding" of racism is truly a matter of common sense? How do you interpret the disconnect between the general condemnation of this form of racism on the personal plane and the persistence of personal acts of commonsense racism to this day?

3. How do you understand conversion as a general theological movement? What do you think conversion means in relation to racism, and how might you be called to pursue conversion as part of your own response to racism?

CHAPTER TWO

Social Manifestations of Racism

For many people in the United States today, the question of racism's social or systemic characteristics is a polarizing one, conjuring up vague notions of "critical race theory" that individuals are reflexively primed to either accept or reject based on their preexisting political alignments. For Catholics, however, this should not be a controversial idea, because the notion that racism is not simply lodged in our hearts but also rooted in our social lives is a natural, and even necessary, extension of our tradition's insistence that racism is a form of sin. As long as we start with the eyes of faith, we can transcend the rhetoric that says one's definition of racism is *either* personal or structural, according to one's political allegiances. Instead, we can adopt the classic Catholic "both/and" to affirm that racism is a multifaceted problem rooted in our fallen human tendency to sin, and we can therefore expect to find it in both fallen human beings and fallen human institutions.

The point of this chapter is to unpack these connections and demonstrate that an acknowledgment and critique of racism's social, systemic, or institutional features is not a concession some Catholics make to their personal political convictions but is a response all Catholics are called to embrace as an authentic application of our shared "responsibility of reading the signs of the times and of interpreting them in the light of the Gospel" (*Gaudium et Spes*, no. 4).

The U.S. Catholic Bishops' Teachings
on the Social Dimensions of Racism

The Catholic theological tradition has a variety of resources for talking about the multifaceted manifestations of racism, but I want to begin with the U.S. bishops' analysis of this question because I think their teachings provide a succinct way to highlight the call we share as Catholics to see racism as a *theological* issue. Because I want to encourage us to think theologically, then, I am going to set aside the terms that are typically used in our secular discourse about racism—things like "systemic racism," "institutional racism," and "structural racism"—and talk simply about the "social dimensions of racism" when describing the general phenomenon of racism as a problem that transcends personal attitudes and actions alone.

To be clear, this linguistic decision should not be interpreted as a denial of the phenomena the more conventional language is meant to describe. On the contrary (as I hope will become apparent in this chapter), there is a real alignment between the experiences these terms strive to capture and the Catholic diagnosis of racism, which readily affirms that racism can indeed become lodged in social systems, institutions, and structures. Before we can address any of these elements, though, we must appreciate the broader claim behind all these terms—namely, that racism is not limited to the individual acts of personal agents but has the potential to exist on a social level. And, just as important, I think we need to explore that broader claim in a theological fashion, and that is why I use the language of the "social dimensions of racism."

As it happens, the U.S. Catholic bishops have pastoral letters on racism that speak directly to the social dimensions of this sin. In the 1979 *Brothers and Sisters to Us*, for instance, the bishops argue that "racism and economic oppression are distinct but interrelated forces which dehumanize our society." The result, they argue, is the creation and maintenance of divergent economic opportunities for different racial groups that reflect "an unresolved racism that permeates our society's structures and resides in the hearts of many among the majority." In their account, this social dimension of racism is both systemic and structural because "the educational, legal, and financial *systems*, along with *other structures and sectors of our society*, impede people's progress and narrow their access because they are black, Hispanic, Native American, or Asian" (emphasis added). Indicting the way "the structures of our society are subtly racist" for promoting "the success of the majority and the failure of the minority," the bishops maintain that a collective form of sin is involved and argue that "the sin is social in nature in that each of us, in varying degrees, is responsible."

Lest we assume that the bishops' theological account of racism as a social (and not just personal) sin is a peculiar feature of the 1970s, it is important to note that the bishops reaffirm their diagnosis in 2018. In fact, the bishops stress even more explicitly that "racism comes in many forms" (*Open Wide Our Hearts*, 4). Specifically, they assert that, in addition to the personal manifestations of racism "found in our hearts" and discussed in the previous chapter of this book, "racism can also be institutional, when practices or traditions are upheld that treat certain groups of people unjustly" (5). They add, "We have also seen years of systemic racism working in how resources are allocated to communities that remain *de facto* segregated" (6). They also draw a direct line between the sins of the past and our contemporary battles with racism, arguing that all Catholics must "examine where the racist attitudes of yesterday have become a permanent part of our perceptions, practices, and policies of today, or how they have been enshrined in our social, political, and economic structures" (16).

Between these two documents, there should be no doubt that the Catholic theological evaluation of racism is not one that bristles at or otherwise rejects the claim, seemingly so controversial in current political discourse, that racism has social dimensions. Indeed, the U.S. Catholic bishops have been quick to note that the social dimensions of racism are variously manifest in the social systems, institutions, and structures that define our shared life in this country. Catholics cannot, therefore, dismiss larger conversations about systemic racism, institutional racism, and structural racism and attempt to restrict the discussion to the interpersonal acts of personal agents alone. On the contrary, Catholics are called to join this conversation wholeheartedly, for we not only share the basic assumptions but have an added responsibility to do something about the persistence of racism at the social level, where "the sinfulness is often anonymous but nonetheless real" (*Brothers and Sisters to Us*).

The bishops' analysis of the social dimensions of racism does more than simply affirm that Catholics should acknowledge the ways racism can be identified in social systems, institutions, and structures. It also provides an added rationale for an increased Catholic effort to wrestle with the social dimensions of racism. Specifically, the bishops' comments situate the social dimensions of racism in the Catholic theological tradition and allow us to confront the systemic, institutional, and structural forms of racism not as a generic social problem but as a particular illustration of sin.

This theological assessment has two practical implications. First, it heightens the importance of counteracting the social dimensions of racism. As the Catholic moral theologian Darlene Fozard Weaver reminds us, what makes a sin a "sin" and not just some generalized bad occurrence or unfortunate outcome "is its distinctively theological referent, estrangement from God," because sin is diametrically opposed to God's nature and will.[1] To call something a sin, then, is to impose the weight of divine judgment upon it, to declare that this thing separates us from God and creates a condition that is not as God would have intended. We, as a people of faith, cannot sit idly while sin persists, because we undermine the will of God if we do. Stressing the sinful features of the social dimensions of racism thus reminds us that we have a theological obligation "to begin to change policies and structures that allow racism to persist" (*Open Wide Our Hearts*, 18).

Second, characterizing the social dimensions of racism as a sin provides added tools for developing a productive response. By recognizing racism as a social sin, we can make use of the concepts in Catholic moral theology that explain the social dimensions of sin more broadly, allowing us to better pinpoint the foundations of the social manifestations of racism and more effectively target our actions at those roots. This project is, in essence, the point of the remaining three parts of this book. Before we get to that more detailed analysis, however, we need a more complete account of the sinful elements of the social dimensions of racism. For the final section of this chapter, then, I will explore how the social dimensions of racism function as a form of sin, using both the U.S. Catholic bishops' perspective and the interpretations of Fr. Bryan Massingale, the Catholic priest and moral theologian introduced in chapter 1.

The Social Dimensions of Racism and Sin

An important starting point for analyzing the sinful elements of the social dimensions of racism is a recognition of the close link between personal and social sin. In the Catholic tradition, any social sin is always "the result of the accumulation and concentration of many personal sins" (*Reconciliatio et Paenitentia*, no. 16).[2] Building on this connection, the U.S. Catholic bishops stress that the social dimensions of racism emerge because "the cumulative effects of personal sins of racism have led to social structures of injustice and violence that make us all accomplices in racism [See *Catechism of the Catholic Church*, no. 1869]" (*Open Wide Our Hearts*, 5). Their account means that, in the Catholic understanding, the social dimensions of racism are intricately linked to the personal manifestations of racism. There is not a neat split between these two planes but an intrinsic connection that requires a multifaceted response. One must never lose sight of the fact that any effort to address the social dimensions of racism must be accompanied by the process of personal conversion discussed in chapter 1.

The clearest way to appreciate the link between the personal and social planes in the sin of racism is to recall the social influence on conscience that has allowed the commonsense definition of racism described in the last chapter to become more commonly condemned. This change was possible because our consciences are not formed in a vacuum, and this fact means that we must think about both the social assumptions that are shaping our own individual consciences and the ways that the errant judgments of others' consciences shape our social assumptions. The U.S. Catholic bishops talk about this interaction when they note that racism is not just "found in the hearts of individuals who can be dismissed as ignorant or unenlightened. But racism still profoundly affects our culture" (*Open Wide Our Hearts*, 6).

Fr. Massingale's theological research offers a similar diagnosis and helps us better appreciate what this aspect of racism means in practice. A frequent critic of "cultural sin," especially in relation to racism, Fr. Massingale has argued that a cultural form of racism has become entrenched in the United States. He explains that culture can be understood as "the sets of meanings and values that inform a people's way of life,"[3] meaning that we can see culture most easily in the assumptions that a given group is willing to take at face value, without demanding evidence to back them up. Because these claims go unquestioned, they have the ability to shape not only the values but also the actions of the people who share the same culture. A cultural form of racism is thus one that aligns certain value judgments with certain racial identities, suggesting one racial group is more trustworthy or less threatening or otherwise more valuable than another. These values then form the people who live in that culture, prompting members of the valorized group to think more of themselves and less of others while promoting the opposite conclusion for anyone who identifies with another racial group.[4]

In the U.S. context, this cultural conditioning has emphasized the value of White individuals and contradicted the inherent worth of Black, Latino, Native American, and Asian peoples. A classic example would be the vicious rhetoric used not infrequently in the context of U.S. political debates about immigration laws, which casually merges immigrant status and Mexican ethnicity and then further connects both to suspicions of criminality. The unstated assumptions in these equations are then used to assert that someone who is White does not need to have their citizenship status questioned, but someone who appears to be Latino must produce immigration papers at a moment's notice. When challenged about this unequal treatment, proponents argue that it is a necessary inconvenience to ensure "law and order," but this argument simply reveals the power of cultural racism, for scholars note that there is an "immigrant paradox, whereby first-generation immigrants display better behavioral outcomes than native-born Americans and more highly acculturated immigrants despite the relative socioeconomic disadvantages and risk factors that immigrants face."[5] In other words, the people our culture prefers to label as "criminals" are the ones who are least likely to commit crimes. Despite its incongruity with the facts, the cultural narrative persists because we choose to embrace what Fr. Massingale calls a "cultured indifference" that gives "the benefit of the doubt" and the "presumption of innocence" to White individuals and imposes the "assumption of guilt" on anyone who is not seen as White according to our social conventions.[6]

The assumptions behind this race-based cultural indifference have negative effects on the relationships between different racial groups, primarily by encouraging White individuals to assume the disparate treatment of Blacks, Latinos, Native Americans, and Asians is not a major concern. Hence, when news reports describe the prevalence of racial profiling in the retail industry, many White Americans might criticize the tactic, but few feel the need to do anything concrete to challenge the practice. Rather than recognizing, as St. Paul said, that we are all members of the Body of Christ and accepting that "[i]f [one] part suffers, all the parts suffer with it" (1 Cor 12:26), White Catholics overall tend to adopt the same cultured indifference that says this is not "my" problem. It is therefore understandable that our bishops would insist, in a quote cited in the last chapter, that "racism can often be found in our hearts—in many cases placed there unwillingly or unknowingly *by our upbringing and culture*" (*Open Wide Our Hearts*, 5, emphasis added). They are speaking to the ways we all too easily adopt the presuppositions of our broader U.S. culture. They are reminding us of the social dimensions of racism.

Given the convictions of our faith, Catholics will naturally want to find ways to challenge this cultural racism. If it is indeed a form of sin, as Fr. Massingale stresses, then we cannot continue our complicity in good conscience. One part of the response should be the personal conversion discussed in chapter 1, because we are not slaves to our cultural influences. We can choose how to respond to the values our culture teaches, and we must take responsibility for our willingness to accept the cultured indifference of racism when we could be consciously questioning these assumptions.

Personal conversion alone will not be enough, however, for the cultural form of racism that Fr. Massingale explains and that the U.S. Catholic bishops critique does not just happen on its own. Instead, a whole system of structural influences supports and reinforces the cultured indifference that gives White people the benefit of the doubt while pretending to legitimate the pall of suspicion it casts on everyone else. As a result, the Catholic confrontation of racism needs to extend to the very structures of our society so that we can recognize what our bishops underscore: "Many of our institutions still harbor, and too many of our laws still sanction, practices that deny justice and equal access to certain groups of people. God demands more from us" (*Open Wide Our Hearts*, 10).

Conclusion

When we recognize the social dimensions of racism that the U.S. Catholic bishops have consistently presented as a logical extension of racism's sinful nature, we can see that God demands more from us than the personal conversion we are also called to prioritize in response to the sins of commonsense racism. To prioritize personal conversion alone, without attending to and dismantling the institutions, laws, and other structures that deny justice, would be like telling someone whose furnace is broken that they can make it through the winter just fine if they put on a sweater and think warm thoughts. They might be able to buy enough clothes to insulate themselves from the cold, but they would have a lot more success if they coupled this strategy with an effort to fix the physical structure in their house that could change the environment around them.

Similarly, our Catholic tradition, with its recognition of the social dimensions of racism, tells us that we need to take the steps to reshape our social environment when we are hoping to improve our personal moral "temperature." Much like the person with added layers but no heat, we may be able to insulate our thoughts from the perverse values in the cultural air around us, but we will still have to fight against the cold judgments and racist assumptions that are reinforced by our shared practices. We will have much greater success if we do not have to fight those headwinds but can instead work to form our consciences in a context that promotes the good values we are trying to internalize. As the U.S. Catholic bishops explain, "The roots of racism have extended deeply into the soil of our society," so "racism can only end if we contend with the policies and institutional barriers that perpetuate and preserve the inequality" (*Open Wide Our Hearts*, 28).

The means to this end can also come from within our shared Catholic moral tradition. By mining the depths of Catholic teachings on the social dimensions of sin, especially the notion of structural sin, we can arrive at a better sense of the specific mechanisms by which the social dimensions of racism operate in our society. Such is the task for part II.

Questions for Reflection and Discussion

1. To what extent are you familiar with the terms "systemic racism," "institutional racism," and "structural racism"? What is your reaction to the fact that U.S. Catholic bishops have consistently acknowledged the social dimensions of racism to which these terms allude?

2. How would you define the nature of the sin involved in the social dimensions of racism? What does the theological category of sin add to the conversation about racism's social influences?

3. In what ways does your experience confirm or complicate Fr. Massingale's description of cultural racism? How might you find ways to incorporate the experiences of others—particularly those who have a different racial identity—into your evaluation of this phenomenon?

PART II

Structural Racism as Structural Sin

Accepting that the Catholic obligation to confront racism needs to proceed on both the personal and the social planes, part II examines how Catholic moral theology understands the function of sinful influences at the social level so that Catholics can better understand and respond to the social dimensions of racism. This task is essential because there is not a "commonsense" description of racism at the social level that receives the widely shared recognition of the personal definition. In fact, we are much more likely to contest the idea that social manifestations of racism are even racism, preferring instead to treat any disparities in the treatment of different races as a necessary response to different choices or different starting points that are beyond our control, even when the facts fail to support this interpretation.

New York City's controversial "stop and frisk" policy provides one quick example of this tendency. Proponents of the policy regularly rejected the notion that the program represented a manifestation of racism by asserting that the disproportionate number of Black and Hispanic individuals involved in stops (collectively, 84 percent of stops vs. 50 percent of the New York City population, according to one scholarly analysis of the program) was simply a reflection of greater crime rates among these racial and ethnic groups. When controlling for racial differences in crime rates, however, the stops were still significantly out of proportion, suggesting that what Fr. Bryan Massingale describes as the cultural form of racism was a factor both in the stops themselves and in the defense of the practice.[1]

Given the episcopal teachings about racism discussed in part I, Catholics have the resources to resist these quick dismissals and to acknowledge that racism does in fact have distinct social manifestations. Accepting this idea in the abstract is much different from affirming it in practice, however, and many Catholics—again, especially though not exclusively White Catholics—struggle with the latter. Part II aims to assist with this struggle, drawing on the Catholic account of structural sin to create practical tools for a Catholic theological analysis of the phenomenon our bishops have called us to recognize and combat.

CHAPTER THREE

The Structural Nature
of Structural Sin

When theologians talk about structural sin, they like to talk about water. Although this may seem an unusual place to start, sociologists also frequently use water to illustrate some unique features of social structures, so they have a certain justification. Plus, water is a remarkable compound that illustrates the way individual pieces can combine to generate a whole new thing that is not unreasonably characterized as somehow more than just the sum of its parts. This is essentially what the idea of structural sin is meant to express on the social level.

I am no chemist, so the explanation here is almost certainly rife with scientific errors, but it should be close enough to reality to get the theological point across. Water is composed of two hydrogen atoms and one oxygen atom that combine to form a molecule. This molecule has some peculiar features that distinguish it from its constituent parts. An actual chemist could generate a lengthy list of these features, but I am going to focus on my favorite illustration: fire.

As anyone with a passing interest in aviation history can confirm, hydrogen is a very volatile element. The famed *Hindenburg* disaster is attributed to the rapid ignition of the seven million cubic feet of hydrogen that had been keeping the airship afloat. Much like hydrogen, oxygen is also an especially dangerous element around fires, although not because it burns itself but because it makes other materials ignite more easily. Thus, household fire safety conventions dictate that one should try to smother a cooking oil fire on the stovetop to starve it of oxygen and thereby extinguish the flames. In isolation, then, hydrogen and oxygen are a firefighter's worst nightmare. In the happy combination of two hydrogen atoms per oxygen atom, however, they are the firefighter's essential tool. I know it makes sense as a scientific fact, but it still blows my mind that the water we rely on most to put out fires is made up of two of the things we would least want to have around a fire.

The point of this simplistic foray into the scientific world is to show a common reality that we do not appreciate often enough; namely, individual components can work together in such a way that they create a whole new entity that behaves differently from, and sometimes independently of, the pieces that brought it into existence in the first place. Sociologists talk about this process in the social, rather than chemical, realm using the term "emergence" because they aim to highlight how a new thing *emerges* from an assembly of constituent parts (again, think water "emerging" from hydrogen and oxygen).

Catholic moral theologians use the idea of emergence to insist that it is not only appropriate but also necessary to talk about structures of sin, or structural sin (I use the terms interchangeably), as its own distinct phenomenon even though it is necessarily linked, in the Catholic understanding of human moral agency, back to the actions of personal agents. The idea of emergence explains how the Congregation for the Doctrine of the Faith, the Vatican office responsible for safeguarding the integrity of Catholic teaching on matters of faith and morals, can say simultaneously that structures of sin "are the result of man's actions . . . [and have] the root of [their] evil . . . in free and responsible persons" while also affirming that such structures "often tend to become fixed and fossilized as mechanisms relatively independent of the human will."[1] In essence, they are saying about structures exactly what we see in the case of water, which is that individual elements—here, personal actions and, more precisely, personal sins—can combine to create a new reality that has the capacity to function in a manner that goes beyond what its components might do on their own.

It is these distinct functions of the structures of sin after they have "emerged" from personal sins that we need to understand if we want to arrive at a fuller appreciation of the Catholic account of racism as a sin that has both personal and social dimensions. As St. John Paul II proclaimed in his own defense of the language of "structures of sin," we "cannot easily gain a profound understanding of the reality that confronts us unless we give a name to the root of the evils which afflict us" (*Sollicitudo Rei Socialis*, no. 36).[2] The Catholic name for that root is structural sin, and this concept is an especially fruitful tool for the Catholic evaluation of racism today. Before we can explore what this concept means in the context of racism, however, we need to have a clearer account of the concept on its own terms. The point of this chapter, therefore, is to explain the notion of structural sin in Catholic moral theology.

The Catholic Account of Structural Sin

The concept of structural sin has played a role in Catholic moral theology since the 1960s, when the Latin American bishops' experience with their flocks led them to argue that injustices ingrained in social structures were sinful in a particular way that was not adequately captured by pointing solely to the personal sins that might have created the structures in the first place.[3] The concept subsequently received ample attention during the papacy of John Paul II, as he used the term "structures of sin" to criticize large-scale forces like the ideological blocs of East and West dividing the Cold War world (*Sollicitudo Rei Socialis*, nos. 36–37) and the "culture of death" that was eroding respect for the sanctity of life (*Evangelium Vitae*, nos. 12, 24, 59).[4] In the years since, theologians have worked to articulate a more precise definition of structural sin by focusing on what makes something a social structure in the first place. This work—spearheaded by, among others, Daniel K. Finn at St. John's School of Theology and Seminary in Minnesota—has yielded three key insights that are now regularly employed by Catholic moral theologians: (1) structures emerge from relational connections, (2) structures influence actions and shape outcomes, and (3) structures can be ordered to good or evil.

1. Structures Emerge from Relational Connections

As a complex entity, structures are assembled from smaller parts that are combined to make a larger whole. Because structures are a social phenomenon, they rely on the most basic building blocks of social life: relationships. Finn uses technical sociological language to identify social structures more specifically in the "systems of human relations among social positions," but we can see his point in the simple idea that any time we link a bunch of people in some social context, a web of human connections emerges, stitching the individual people and their relationships together in a new way.[5] The term "social structure" allows us to talk about this web of relationships so that we can better evaluate the effect those connections have on the people who are linked within the web.

To give a more concrete example, my family is a kind of social structure that emerges from the particular way in which I am related to my children as their father and my wife as her husband. Each of these positions has a series of social expectations attached to it, which is part of what it means to describe them as "social positions." If we think of each of these roles as its own "element," then our family becomes the (water) molecule that emerges from the particular way in which we have linked the three elements of father, mother, and children. And, much like water, this new "compound" family has a way of interacting with the world around it that is distinct from the way any one of us might interact with the world were we not bonded together in this particular manner.

The Catholic concept of structural sin is meant to call attention to the ways in which our relational connections interact to create broader networks of connection that influence our day-to-day lives. It is meant to remind us that we do not live in a vacuum but are "called from the very beginning to life in society" because we are created by God "to be a 'social being'" (*Compendium of the Social Doctrine of the Church*, no. 149). Whenever we fulfill this calling and interact with one another in social life, we create connections. When we create connections, social structures emerge. The reality of these social structures indicates why it is important for Catholics to consider things like the social dimension of racism: because social structures represent a real force that emerges from the relational connections between social beings.

2. Structures Influence Actions and Shape Outcomes

The Catholic account of structural sin hinges not only on the existence of social structures as emergent entities but also on the idea that these new webs of relational connections can influence actions and shape outcomes. On one level, this is an intuitive claim. A man who is a father reacts differently to a job offer in another city than that same man would as a single individual. Even if he ultimately makes the same choice and, say, decides to move, he will think about the costs and benefits involved differently in light of the relational connections in which he is embedded as a father than he would if he did not live within these links. His family, a social structure emerging from a series of relationships that include him, impacts his choices, influences his actions, and shapes (but does not directly determine) the outcome.

By building on the work of social scientists, Finn has proposed a more precise explanation for how the social structures that emerge from relational connections can have these effects. Citing Margaret Archer, a leading sociologist who advised the Vatican for years as a member and the eventual president of the Pontifical Academy of Social Sciences, Finn argues that the "restrictions, enablements, and incentives" built into the connections between relationships influence people's decisions, often prompting them to choose different things than they might choose if they were not part of those relationships and embedded in those social bonds.

Let me shift gears and describe this facet of social structures using a different illustration. When someone goes out to eat at a restaurant, they are embedded in a structure that revolves around the relative relationship of "patrons" and "servers." Their interactions at the restaurant are shaped by the relational connection between these two roles and by the way patrons and servers are connected to other individuals like friends and bosses, respectively. These connections typically function to keep the dining experience running smoothly. On one side, patrons can expect that they will be able to place their order, that their servers will deliver the food that was requested, and that all this will happen in a timely fashion. On the other side, servers can similarly anticipate that patrons will treat them with respect, that patrons will tip according to local customs, and that patrons will leave when their meal is done to make room for another party.

Most of the time, both patrons and servers live up to these expectations, but Finn would say this is not simply because they are all nice people (though hopefully they are). A relevant factor encouraging both parties to follow the script is the fact that each has something to gain from doing so and something to lose from departing from it. For patrons, if they treat their server with disrespect, they will be at the server's mercy when it comes to the timing of their meal and its ultimate quality (Is this burger extra spicy or is it just me?). The server's social position places some powerful restrictions on the patron's behavior such that the patron might have a lot to lose if they stop behaving thoughtfully in the restaurant.

On the flipside, servers are keenly aware of the incentive they have to please their patrons. At least in the United States, where tipping is common, servers have the potential to gain a noticeable boost to their paycheck when their patrons end their meals in happy spirits. Most servers hustle on the job due, at least in part, to their desire to secure the most lucrative tip possible. Of course, patrons can also refuse to tip, so there is a way in which each incentive is also a restriction, at least insofar as it can be removed entirely.

This example highlights two important things about the nature of social structures and thus, by extension, the nature of structural sin. First, both servers and patrons maintain their agency even when their interactions are constrained by the way they are related to each other through their social roles. The thought that a server could spit in someone's food will not *make* a patron speak more nicely, but it might make them think twice before sounding off in the server's face. The real but not deterministic power of social structures is a significant observation for Catholics, given our steadfast conviction that every human "is created with free will and is master over his acts" (*Catechism of the Catholic Church*, no. 1730).[6] If we were to say that social structures forced people to do certain things in a way that predetermined specific outcomes, we would contradict this claim and eviscerate moral responsibility. Precisely because this vision of social structures stresses restrictions and enablements, it leaves room for humans to choose how to respond in their freedom, affirming the role of free will.

Second, the costs and benefits embedded in the connections between different social positions are not all created equal. The theoretical risks a patron faces are not only a lot less certain but also less immediately impactful than the real risk of lost wages with which servers must constantly contend. Although social structures can never compel someone to act in a certain way because individuals always maintain their freedom, as imbalances in the two parties' incentives and restrictions increase, some outcomes become far more likely than others because most people are simply unwilling to pay the costs associated with doing what they might otherwise want to do.

So far, this illustration has been fairly benign, so it might be a little hard to see how this understanding of social structure helps to shed light on structural sin, let alone the social dimensions of racism. The third claim about structures advanced in the Catholic discussion of structural sin helps to close this gap.

3. Structures Can Be Ordered to Good or Evil
If Catholic theologians like Finn are correct and social structures not only emerge from relationships but also influence actions

and shape outcomes, then it will matter greatly what kinds of be-haviors specific structures reward with incentives and enablements and which ones they discourage with restrictions. When they encourage good outcomes, we might think of the structures that emerge from the connections between relationships as a good thing, creating "structures of grace" that make it easier to do what is right.[7] When they actively encourage bad outcomes, however, social structures become sinful because they make it easier to do what one should not and harder to do what one should. These are the structures of sin that the *Compendium of the Social Doctrine of the Church* explains can become rooted in society and "grow stronger, spread and become sources of other sins, conditioning human conduct" (no. 119).

At the structural level, then, one important task for Catholic moral theology is to help people distinguish between the structures that are oriented to good and those that are oriented to evil. While this may seem like a self-evident distinction, theologians are quick to note that obfuscation, or the ability to make it difficult for us to properly recognize and understand what is happening around us, is an integral part of the operation of sin at the social level, where it creates a "'tissue of lies' placed before our eyes so that we fail to see reality."[8] To counter this danger, we must rely on objective standards to discern good and evil, which is precisely what the Catholic moral tradition offers. According to these standards, a structure will be acting in our best interest when it promotes what St. John Paul II characterized as humanity's "*true good . . .* [or] the voluntary ordering of the person toward his ultimate end: God" (*Veritatis Splendor*, no. 72, emphasis in original).[9] By con-trast, sinful structures will be the ones that move us away from this true good. In the most direct terms, this means structures are problematic whenever a web of relational connections encourages us to be selfish, because this frustrates our fundamental calling to find ways to give ourselves selflessly to others, just as Christ did on the cross (see *Gaudium et Spes*, no. 24).

The fact that structures can be oriented to good or evil means there is no guarantee that social structures will ascribe costs only to antisocial behaviors and attach incentives exclusively to prosocial ones. In fact, if we take humanity's fallen state seriously, we might well assume the opposite—namely, that we would be likely to design our incentives to reward bad behaviors and our restrictions to undermine good ones, even if we do so unintentionally. When these kinds of structures emerge, the result is a structure of sin that makes it easier for people to do the wrong thing and harder to do the right thing. Individual agents can, of course, reject these influences, but given the natural tendency to follow the path of least resistance, we should hardly be surprised that a society whose web of relational connections includes these perverse incentives would be a society in which people more frequently commit the sins for which they are rewarded and less frequently achieve the good from which they are deterred.

Conclusion

The fundamental claim at the heart of the Catholic understanding of structural sin is the idea that our relationships create social webs (structures) that influence our moral choices and actions. Put simply, the way we are connected to others in our various social bonds creates distinct expectations about how we should act, and we experience these expectations as a series of costs and benefits associated with different courses of action. If we want to maintain our social positions, we will tend to act in accord with these expectations, for we necessarily pay a price for transgressing them. None of these influences determines our actions, but they can make it prohibitively difficult to pursue certain options, either directly, by creating dramatic costs for the action in question, or indirectly, by so heavily incentivizing another choice that any other option pales in comparison. When these costs and benefits make it particularly challenging to pursue good actions or dramatically easier to choose sinful ones, then we can see a structure of sin emerging, and our need to challenge that structure of sin arises right along with it.

The category of structural sin thus provides a decidedly Catholic way of interpreting the sinful aspects of the social dimensions of racism and suggests a plausible mechanism by which the cultured indifference defined in chapter 2 can be perpetuated over time. The next chapter will detail this mechanism and demonstrate how the Catholic understanding of structural sin can help us recognize and respond to the social dimensions of racism.

Questions for Reflection and Discussion

1. In what ways do you see structures emerging from your relational connections? Which structures (webs of relationships) are the most important in your life?

2. How do you react to the idea that the restrictions, enablements, and incentives of sinful social structures do not shape our decisions deterministically, because we retain the ability to resist those influences with our free will? What do you think would make some of these influences easier or harder to resist?

3. What kinds of connections do you see between this description of sinful social structures and the presentation of the social dimensions of racism in the last chapter? What might it look like for social structures to influence choices and shape outcomes in a racist fashion?

CHAPTER FOUR

The Sinful Function
of Structural Sin

In 1971, Philip Zimbardo, a psychologist at Stanford University, launched one of the most (in)famous experiments in the history of academic psychology. Curious about the way situational circumstances affect behavior, Zimbardo recruited a small team of volunteer participants and re-created a prison by randomly assigning half to be prisoners and half to be guards. The "prisoners" were arrested and brought to a mock prison, where Zimbardo instructed the "guards" simply to do what they needed to do to keep the "prison" running efficiently.

Rather quickly, both sides settled into their respective roles. To assert their power during the first night, the guards decided to wake the prisoners at 2:30 in the morning. When the prisoners tried to rebel, the guards separated and humiliated them, and the prisoners became increasingly passive and obedient. The guards, meanwhile, behaved more and more authoritatively, creating arbitrary rules and inflicting harsh psychological punishments. Eventually, Zimbardo's colleagues convinced him to intervene before things got irreversibly out of hand. As Zimbardo later explained, "Our planned two-week investigation into the psychology of prison life had to be ended after only six days because of what the situation was doing to the college students who participated.

In only a few days, our guards became sadistic and our prisoners became depressed and showed signs of extreme stress."[1]

Notably, all this happened with a group of participants who had been carefully screened and intentionally selected for their prosocial tendencies and lack of antisocial behaviors. How did this good group go bad so quickly? For Zimbardo and his colleagues, "the extremely pathological reactions which emerged in both groups of subjects testif[ied] to the power of the social forces operating."[2] The guards were doing terrible things not because they were terrible people but because they took on a specific role that connected them to other humans in a distinct way, and these connections began to shape the way they saw themselves to the point that they acted in a manner they would not have acted under more normal circumstances. In other words, Zimbardo and his team inadvertently showcased the power social structures have to negatively influence individual agents, ultimately encouraging them to act in ways that contradict the call to "love your neighbor as yourself" (Matt 22:39). They illustrated structural sin in action.

The Stanford Prison Experiment thus helps to explain why Catholics cannot sit idly by in a world shaped by structures of sin. Because these structures can so dramatically—and so rapidly—shift individuals' behaviors and encourage them to act in cruel ways they would not even have considered on their own, structures of sin represent a grave threat to the common good. While this is true in general, it is particularly applicable in the context of racism, where structures of sin have the potential to steer otherwise good and kind people toward racial discrimination, creating a social environment that directly undermines what St. John Paul II called "the good of all and of each individual" (*Sollicitudo Rei Socialis*, no. 38). This chapter delves more deeply into the Catholic understanding of structural sin, first, to clarify how sinful social structures can have this alarming impact and, second, to explain the particular nature of this impact on the social dimensions of racism.

From Sinful Social Structures to Sinful Personal Actions

We have already seen how Catholic moral theologians see social structures influencing actions and shaping outcomes through the restrictions, enablements, and incentives they present to the actors who interact with them. What is not yet clear, however, is why individual moral agents would respond to these restrictions, enablements, and incentives in this way. Why would we even be susceptible to a structure that adds a cost or introduces a benefit? How can these abstract offers ultimately affect our decisions?

The answer has to do with the way we make moral judgments and then translate those judgments into action. In recent years, neuroscientists and moral psychologists have added new details to our understanding of this process, suggesting that our knowledge of right and wrong is a kind of capacity that can change over time. Using fMRI machines, these researchers have identified the specific areas of our brains that are involved in moral judgments. Based on these data, they have concluded that effective moral judgments rely on both emotional reactions in the more "affective" parts of our brains and reasoned evaluations in the more strictly "cognitive" parts.

The two main proponents of this work, Joshua D. Greene of Harvard University and Jonathan Haidt of New York University's Stern School of Business, have slightly different interpretations of how these two parts of our brain interact when making moral judgments. Greene argues that every moral judgment essentially runs through a two-step process. In one step, our brains make an affective judgment, and in the next step, our brains make a rational assessment. When these two things align, we make judgments swiftly and easily. Hence, it does not take me long to conclude that I really should not take a second sample from the table at the grocery story with the "Please take *one*" sign on it because I feel on the gut level that this would be wrong, and my more calculated judgments would likewise affirm that this would indeed be inappropriate. When the two processes conflict, however, we must deliberate further to decide whether we want to go with our gut or our reason. Sometimes our cognitive reflection will overrule our affective intuition, but most of the time, Greene explains, our gut wins out.[3]

Haidt likewise emphasizes a sort of two-step process, but he believes that one step runs the show. According to his interpretation, we always start with an affective intuition, and then we simply use our cognitive reasoning capacities to find the most acceptable ways to articulate the judgment of our intuition. We do not engage in a reasoned deliberation at all; instead, we make a judgment based on intuition and then merely use our cognitive processes to rationalize our intuitive judgment after the fact.[4]

Obviously, Greene and Haidt have competing explanations about how our moral judgments work, but they also have a striking point of overlap that helps us appreciate the function of social structures—and, especially, structures of sin—in the moral life. They both stress the importance of our initial affective response. For Haidt, this response is determinative, but even for Greene, it is essential, because although he imagines our intuitive judgment is subject to further review, the intuitive judgment is still the starting point for the cognitive analysis. Like a legal ruling, our intuitive reaction has the benefit of the doubt and will stand as long as it is not overruled.

The upshot of these studies is that getting our moral intuitions right is spectacularly important if we are going to make good moral judgments and act rightly. For Haidt, this is all that matters, and for Greene, this will at least make our lives a lot easier by removing the hurdle of cognitive dissonance. Their work suggests that refining our intuitions must be an important part of our efforts to act rightly. This observation means that we need to attend to *who* we learn from and not just *what* they are trying to teach us.

Although we like to imagine that our intuitive judgments are fundamentally *our* judgments—that is, judgments made by us on a deeply personal level—psychological research reveals that our moral intuitions are deeply influenced by our social environments. As social creatures, we are hardwired through evolutionary processes to have a predisposition for agreeing with the moral judgments of our peers because we can benefit from the social cooperation this agreement generates and sustains. Social structures, then, can have a powerful influence on our moral judgments, and thus our moral actions, when they communicate the values of our social group, because those are the values we are primed to internalize most easily when we form moral intuitions. Because these moral intuitions drive so many of our moral judgments, the restrictions, enablements, and incentives built into our web of relationships have a way of coloring our assessment of what is right and wrong. When they ultimately corrupt that assessment with incorrect moral intuitions, these structures leave us willing to do things that outside observers would swiftly condemn as wrong, because we can no longer see that they are wrong. And thus, we arrive at the behaviors Zimbarbo witnessed in his prison experiment.

The implications for the social dimensions of racism are likely becoming clear. Insofar as the web of connections that emerges from our various relationships in society "socially idealizes or economically incentivizes actions seeking exclusive self-interest(s) at the expense of the common good," that social structure becomes a structure of sin that interrupts the proper formation of our moral intuitions.[5] When we do exactly what we are prepped by centuries of human development to do and latch on to these erroneous intuitions, we put ourselves one step closer to sinful actions. We might, ultimately, override the faulty intuition, but we most likely will not because it would take a new affective judgment to override our first, incorrect intuition. When we are surrounded exclusively by the people who gave us the wrong intuition in the first place, we have very little reason to question that intuition and every incentive not to. When racism is entangled in the restrictions, enablements, and incentives that communicate our society's values to us, we can begin to see how racism—in both its personal and social manifestations—"retreats underground only to keep reemerging," as Pope Francis warns (*Fratelli Tutti*, no. 20). To truly appreciate what all this talk of structural sin means for the social dimensions of racism, though, we must give just a little more thought to how sinful social structures exert their influence in racially discriminatory ways.

Racism and Structural Sin

Put simply, structures of sin become a direct component of the social dimension of racism when the restrictions, enablements, and incentives built into the way people are connected in a specific context function to benefit the collective interests of one racial group at the expense of another group's flourishing. This definition allows us to build on the nuanced understanding of the power of social structures, which has become an important part of the Catholic account of sin's social impacts, so that we can better appreciate the social dimensions of racism as a form of sin. It also highlights the fact that sinful social structures harm the common good because economic incentives and social ideals that help just one racial group contradict the Catholic conviction that the common good "stems from the dignity, unity and equality of all people" (*Compendium of the Social Doctrine of the Church*, no. 164) and is not just at the service of a select few. Furthermore, the Catholic understanding of the common good, described in *Gaudium et Spes* (no. 26), as "the sum total of social conditions which allow people, either as groups or as individuals, to reach their fulfillment more fully and more easily" provides the necessary details for us to distinguish structures that recognize difference in a way that promotes flourishing from those that use racial distinctions to frustrate the well-being of particular groups.

In practical terms, the Catholic account of structural sin means that structures of sin can contribute to the perpetuation of racism at the social level in two distinct but interrelated ways. First, structures of sin can influence individual moral judgments by reinforcing the problematic moral intuitions that amount to what Fr. Bryan Massingale describes as a cultural form of racism (elaborated on in this book in chapter 2).[6] This happens when a sinful social structure sends the message that one racial group is more valuable than another and thereby encourages the people who come into contact with that structure to adopt this racist perspective. Recalling the U.S. Catholic bishops' reminder that "racism arises when—either consciously or unconsciously—a person holds that his or her race or ethnicity is superior, and therefore judges persons of other races or ethnicities as inferior and unworthy of equal regard" (*Open Wide Our Hearts*, 3), we can see a genuine form of racism in this system of perverse incentives and warped ideals. When sinful social structures communicate social support for these racist attitudes, they give racism a structural dimension that capitalizes on the power of a social group's restrictions, enablements, and incentives to shape individuals' moral intuitions. They help these false perspectives about racial inferiority permeate throughout society and even across generations, providing the mechanism by which cultural racism persists.

Beyond the effect on attitudes, structures of sin also have a second impact—on actions—that is just as relevant to the contemporary challenge of racism. Precisely because moral judgments are *practical* judgments, they never remain at the level of abstraction but always have consequences in the realm of action. When sinful social structures actively encourage people to undertake racially discriminatory actions, by socially idealizing or economically incentivizing them, we should properly regard and condemn these structures of sin as a form of racism. In this case, the indictment aligns with the U.S. Catholic bishops' judgment that "racist acts are sinful because they violate justice. They reveal a failure to acknowledge the human dignity of the persons offended, to recognize them as the neighbors Christ calls us to love (Mt 22:39)" (*Open Wide Our Hearts*, 3). By making it easier, or even in some way profitable, for individuals to disadvantage those who happen to be members of a particular racial group, these structures of sin reject the dignity of the neighbors Christ calls us to love. When sinful social structures make these denials of dignity easier to commit and thus more likely to occur, they give racism a social dimension.

These two functions, then, help clarify what it means to speak about the social dimensions of racism in relation to structural sin. They suggest that Catholics should be especially attuned to and critical of sinful social structures that reinforce racially discriminatory attitudes or that promote, via social ideals and economic incentives, racially discriminatory actions. In the next part of this book, we will look at some illustrations of these functions, but before we do that, I want to highlight one final advantage of utilizing the Catholic conception of structural sin in this context.

While there might be lingering resistance to labeling a given web of connections between relationships as a form of racism because of the way we tend to object to the castigation of any one individual as a racist, a distinct advantage of the structural shift is that this does not make every individual who interacts with or lives within a given social structure a racist. There remains a strong distinction in the Catholic perspective between the power social structures exert to shape reality and the choices individual moral agents make within those structures. The Catholic understanding of structural sin underscores this distinction in part by revealing the insufficiency of using appeals to the goodness of individual moral agents to avoid conversations about structural racism.

From this theological perspective, it is not enough to argue that many, or even most, people operating within a sinful social structure are well intentioned, good natured, and not purposefully racist if the structures they inhabit are promoting racist values and facilitating racially discriminatory outcomes, because, as the discussion of moral psychology above emphasized, social structures constantly shape the intuitions and value judgments of the moral agents who come into contact with them. Far from tarnishing the reputation of good people, a theological analysis of the structures of sin promoting racism can serve as a call for everyone to appreciate how difficult it is to live within sinful social structures in a morally uncompromised fashion. It is also a reminder of the shared duty all people have to reform these structures so that it will be easier for individual moral agents to make the right choices.

Conclusion

The main function of this chapter has been to explain in more detail the way social structures, especially sinful social structures, shape moral actions. Insights from moral psychology helped to highlight the power of moral intuitions in our moral judgments and, thus, our moral actions. The social nature of those intuitions then provided a way to recognize how social structures can influence moral actions by sending a message about the moral intuitions one should adopt in the first place. This account then informed the specification of two ways sinful social structures can contribute to the perpetuation of racism in society when they benefit the collective interests of one racial group at the expense of another. Their function occurs either at the level of attitudes, where structures of sin can encourage individuals to adopt the intuitive judgment that one racial group is superior to another or that one or more racial groups is inherently inferior, or at the level of action, where structures of sin can promote discriminatory actions themselves. Altogether, the analysis in this chapter means that Catholics should heed the call to respond to the social dimensions of racism by looking out for social structures that reinforce racially discriminatory attitudes or that incentivize racially discriminatory actions. As the next part will discuss, there is no shortage of opportunities for Catholics to pursue this responsibility today.

Questions for Reflection and Discussion

1. What do you make of the insight that moral intuitions play a fundamental role in our moral judgments? How would you characterize the role of intuition in your own moral judgment based on your experiences with trying to discern how to respond to a specific moral question?

2. How would you define a racist structure of sin? What would you want to add to or remove from this chapter's assertion that a racist structure of sin arises "when the restrictions, enablements, and incentives built into the way people are connected in a specific context function to benefit the collective interests of one racial group at the expense of another"?

3. To what extent do you agree with this chapter's closing assertion that the Catholic account of structural sin helps us assess the social dimensions of racism without requiring an indictment of each of the individual agents who operate within racist structures of sin? Is this more of an asset or a liability for the analysis?

PART III

Racism as Structural Sin Today

Part III explores four significant areas where the social dimensions of racism can be seen in structures of sin in the United States even today. The first chapter discusses the way legal structures associated with policing and housing have functioned to reinforce racist attitudes and to encourage racially discriminatory actions, making it difficult for good people to do the good they long to do as a result of a fraught history that connects policing and housing with racist forms of structural sin. The second chapter discusses more informal institutional norms in the realm of healthcare and higher education that similarly function to encourage and facilitate racially discriminatory outcomes that deny the equal and inherent dignity of all racial groups.

In all four cases, the analysis complements rather than contradicts the U.S. Catholic bishops' reflections on the social dimensions of racism. They readily lament the fact that "all too often, Hispanics and African Americans, for example, face discrimination in hiring, housing, educational opportunities, and incarceration" shortly before noting that "racism can also be institutional" (*Open Wide Our Hearts*, 4–5). The discussion in Part III can simply be read as adding specificity to their claims so that we can better respond to these injustices from the heart of our faith.

CHAPTER FIVE

Policing and Housing

Any discussion of the structural forms of racism in the United States must attend to the fact that the laws of this nation have been a structure of sin with racist implications for much of our history. Thankfully, the worst of these laws have been changed, but this does not alter the fact that our legal structures were originally designed to create restrictions, enablements, and incentives that benefited one racial group at the expense of other groups' flourishing. This is not meant to be a judgmental screed against the history and development of the United States. Rather, it is meant to be an honest reminder that, for all the progress we have made toward our ideals of "liberty and justice for all," the fundamental reason we had to make progress at all was because we started with a rigid form of inequality built into our governing structures. From slavery in the antebellum South to the affirmation of legalized racial segregation by *Plessy v. Ferguson*, our laws regularly put White people in a better position than people who were identified as members of other racial groups, and we still grapple with the ripple effects of this history to this day.

The point of this chapter is to examine two areas where the ripple effects of legalized discrimination are most poignantly impactful. The first is policing, where the legacy of legalized discrimination, and the cultural forms of racism it sustained, interacts with existing laws to create a structure of sin with racially discriminatory implications. The second area is housing, where a failure to grapple with the consequences of prior laws has left structural barriers in the way. In each case, the theological understanding of structural sin helps us appreciate how the social dimensions of racism have taken on a structural form that perpetuates injustice and frustrates the common good.

Racism and Structures of Sin in Policing

One of the contemporary institutions most frequently indicted in current conversations about systemic racism is policing. The indictment is based on the alarming frequency with which interactions between police and people of color, especially Black men, turn violent and even deadly. In response to a series of high-profile cases spanning the geographic breadth of the country—including those of Oscar Grant in Oakland, California; Michael Brown in Ferguson, Missouri; Eric Garner in New York City; Breonna Taylor in Louisville, Kentucky; George Floyd in Minneapolis, Minnesota; and many more both in between and since—observers in the United States have been increasingly unsatisfied with a strictly personalized interpretation of police brutality that attributes each of these incidents to the poor choices of individual officers. Instead, people have argued that there is a flaw in the way policing itself operates that makes these lethal incidents more likely to occur. They are, in essence, claiming that there is a structure of sin influencing police work in the United States to the detriment of people of color.

Given the description of structural sin's impact on racism, Catholics can assess this claim by asking, first, whether there are racially discriminatory outcomes in policing and, second, whether there are any restrictions, enablements, and incentives built into the way police officers are connected to the citizens they police that would support these outcomes, either by encouraging attitudes of racial discrimination or by facilitating racial discrimination in action more directly.

With respect to the first question, there are notable racial disparities in the use of force by police officers. When controlling for population sizes, "Black men are 2.5 times more likely than white men to be killed by police during their lifetime. And . . . Black people who were fatally shot by police seemed to be twice as likely as white people to be unarmed."[1] Moreover, scholars have shown that these variations are not due to racial differences in crime rates or in the frequency of police interactions.[2] Given these disparities, Catholics (like all people of goodwill) need to interrogate what may be behind the disconnect. Although there are numerous restrictions, enablements, and incentives built into the peculiar relationships connecting police officers with the men, women, and children subject to their jurisdiction that have implications for racial discrimination in policing, for the sake of clarity and brevity, I am going to focus on one specific structure: the legal protections afforded to police officers who kill someone on the job.

Police officers are tasked with protecting the common good, and as such, they are authorized to use force, even lethal force, when necessary. From a Catholic perspective, this authorization is not inherently problematic, for it simply reflects the Catholic Church's recognition that "those holding legitimate authority have the right to repel by armed force aggressors against the civil community entrusted to their charge" (*Catechism of the Catholic Church*, no. 2265). Much depends on the determination of when force is necessary—and how much force is needed—to achieve this end, and this is where the structural supports codified in the law veer toward a structural form of sin.

In the United States, the determination of whether a police officer's use of force is justified is governed by the 1989 Supreme Court decision *Graham v. Connor*, which requires legal proceedings to use "the Fourth Amendment's 'objective reasonableness' standard." More specifically, prosecutors, judges, and juries are instructed that "the 'reasonableness' of a particular use of force must be judged from the perspective of a reasonable officer on the scene."[3] In other words, when an officer uses force against a subject (including lethal force), others are asked to evaluate how they imagine a normal police officer would have reacted in the same situation with the same set of known facts.

In the abstract, this seems like an unobjectionable standard, particularly when we appreciate, as Chief Justice William Rehnquist stresses in his opinion, "that police officers are often forced to make split-second judgments—in circumstances that are tense, uncertain, and rapidly evolving—about the amount of force that is necessary in a particular situation."[4] None of us wants to be held accountable for all the things that the twenty-twenty vision of hindsight might reveal but about which we would have had no way of knowing in the moment. If this were all the objective reasonableness standard did, we might indeed find no reason to object. In practice, however, this legal doctrine has far less objective effects.

In ways the Supreme Court could never have intended, the objective reasonableness standard upheld by *Graham* has functioned as a racist form of structural sin that removes the threat of punishment and legal liability—that is, a restriction—and creates the assurance of legal protection—an enablement—for the use of lethal force against Black men and women. This has occurred because the standard is applied in a larger social context that includes cultural values that have been deeply shaped by the United States' racist past, including its legal support of slavery and segregation. As the theologian Laurie Cassidy explains, the United States' original dependence on slavery necessitated the creation of an artificial "*idea* of the black male . . . [that] was distinct from actual living and breathing black male persons" in order to justify the White enslavement of Black bodies. In the years since, this manufactured idea has been reinforced in conventional discourse and popular culture, resulting in the collective elision of Black men with danger.[5] This assumption has profound implications for the objective reasonableness standard because judges and juries are more apt to accept that the generic, "reasonable" officer would likewise react with force when confronting a Black man in a tense situation, given that the culture around us has "taught us all to see black men as dangerous."[6]

It is hardly surprising that most police killings of unarmed Black men do not result in a prosecution, let alone a conviction, because the legal structures encourage the officers involved to stress that they felt threatened in the interaction and then allow judges and juries to agree with that assessment because of the way Black men are connected with danger in our cultural ethos. If our legal structures required the more precise "substantive due process" standard, for instance, these observers would be asked to determine whether the level of force used was genuinely proportionate to the type of danger involved, not just whether a generic officer would have felt threatened in the same way. By rejecting this standard and insisting instead on the objective reasonableness doctrine, the laws of the United States limit (although they do not eliminate) accountability for officers who kill Black men, removing an important restriction that could chip away at racial disparities in the use of force.

The Catholic theological analysis would therefore challenge the objective reasonableness standard, as it is currently employed, as a structure of sin insofar as its de facto guarantee of law enforcement license reinforces the narrow self-interest of one group at the expense of the broader community's need for greater accountability. The theological indictment cannot rest there, however, for the threat to the common good is not a result of an all-encompassing challenge to the conditions of social life that all social groups need in order to flourish, but an assault on the conditions of the specific social groups defined as racial minorities, most especially Black men and women. In this way, the doctrine of objective reasonableness functions as a racist form of structural sin, serving as a prime example of one way in which, as the U.S. Catholic bishops caution, "the racist attitudes of yesterday have become a permanent part of our perceptions, practices, and policies of today" (*Open Wide Our Hearts*, 16).

Racism and Structures of Sin in Housing

Another area where the racist attitudes of yesterday have become enshrined in our current perceptions, and especially practices, through the structure of the law has been housing. As any high school U.S. history textbook will relay, racial discrimination in housing has been illegal in the United States since the Fair Housing Act was passed as part of the Civil Rights Act of 1968. Nevertheless, residential segregation by race in the United States has remained a persistent fact of life and, by some measures, has actually increased in the last few decades. These divisions are damaging for everyone who lives in segregated neighborhoods because every racial group has worse outcomes—in health, educational attainment, income, and more—than they would have in more integrated environments. Inequality has corrosive effects on the social fabric upon which we all rely in order to succeed.[7] Applying the Catholic understanding of structural sin, this state of affairs constitutes a threat to the common good, so we should ask if there are any perverse incentives built into the structures of our society that would lead to this outcome. Rather unsurprisingly, we can find some if we dig into the history of housing in this country.

If we go back to the 1940s and 1950s, we find that the U.S. government instituted a policy of categorizing the riskiness of mortgage loans according to a neighborhood's racial makeup. They literally drew red lines on the maps to mark off the neighborhoods with more people of color, discouraging banks from loaning to homebuyers in those areas. As a result, this legal institution of "redlining," as it came to be known, created significant incentives to preserve racial segregation in housing even in areas of the country where segregation was not the overt law of the land.

More specifically, the availability of federally insured mortgages for homes in White neighborhoods meant that home prices rose quickly in those neighborhoods. At the other end of the spectrum, families living in redlined neighborhoods found a lack of potential buyers for their homes because banks would not lend money to anyone looking to buy a house in those areas. Whiter, suburban areas could therefore rely on credit, in the form of mortgages, to keep prices high, while areas with fewer White residents had to keep their home prices in line with the amounts buyers could afford to pay in cash. The result was an astronomical return on homeownership in White neighborhoods, where home equity became a reliable investment, contrasted by a near absence of any meaningful appreciation in neighborhoods with Black, Hispanic, Asian, and Native American residents. Not only did this allow White families to amass intergenerational wealth at a rate more than five times that of Hispanic families and nearly eight times that of Black families, but it also had the effect of significantly incentivizing White families to live in White neighborhoods, where they had the highest likelihood of reaping a return on their investment in a home.[8]

Over time, the infrastructure of cities evolved to preserve the concentrated wealth created by this legal structure. School districts were built to keep local tax revenues in local coffers, resulting in dramatic disparities in educational quality across an urban and suburban divide in many cities. Heavy industries and other undesirable facilities were steered toward lower-income neighborhoods because wealthier residents had more political capital to spend to keep polluting projects away from their backyards. Similarly, the highways that were built to give suburban residents easier access to downtown jobs tended to plow through the poorer neighborhoods that had previously been redlined, further depressing their property values. The net effect has been to make the rich communities richer while leaving the poorer communities to stagnate. As these economic effects were layered over the racial divisions redlining created, they created a new form of structural sin that incentivizes the maintenance of a racially unjust status quo.

The problem is not just tied to the reverberations of historical restrictions alone, however. There are additional present-day restrictions that add to these obstacles by reducing or even eliminating less expensive access points in wealthier communities. The most significant of these are zoning laws, as many wealthier municipalities use zoning laws to implement severe restrictions on the number of multifamily homes or apartment buildings that can be built in their neighborhoods. This means that the only way to enter the communities with the finest schools, the nicest parks, and the best services is to buy into a single-family home—and usually an expensive one at that. Ostensibly, this opportunity is open to all people regardless of race, but in practice, it is much more accessible to White families than it is to Black families and

Latino families (as well as Native American and Asian families) because of the intergenerational wealth gap redlining created in the first place.[9]

In the realm of housing, then, one can see racism in the structures of sin that are linked to the legacy of the overtly racist laws of the past and that persist in new ways today. The zoning laws, in particular, function to preserve the status quo of residential segregation not by requiring White, Black, Asian, Hispanic, and Native American residents to live in different neighborhoods but by creating the kinds of financial obstacles for entry into historically White neighborhoods that are disproportionately burdensome for non-White homebuyers. In this sense they impose a restriction even more than they provide an enablement, although there is a way in which they encourage and incentivize White residents to remain in the wealthier neighborhoods too. Much like the structural sin in policing discussed earlier, this structural sin in housing makes racially discriminatory outcomes more likely to occur, not as a result of policies with an overtly racist intent, but due to the way superficially neutral policies interact with broader factors—historical, in the case of housing, as opposed to cultural, in the case of policing—to benefit one racial group at the expense of the full flourishing of other racial groups. It thus represents a racist form of structural sin.

Conclusion

This chapter has focused on two important areas at the heart of racial disparities in the United States today, policing and housing, to show how the theological concept of structural sin can help Catholics appreciate the social dimensions of racism in these realms. Admittedly, the examples have been narrow, chiefly addressing one major structural sin that contributes to racially discriminatory outcomes in each area. What the illustrations all show, however, is that the problem of structural forms of racism is not limited to the past alone. Precisely because of the ways our past included overt forms of racism at the systemic level, contemporary social structures with seemingly neutral restrictions, enablements, and incentives are not so neutral in practice. On the contrary, the very restrictions, enablements, and incentives they present today function to benefit one racial group at the expense of the flourishing of other racial groups. They therefore present a contemporary reminder that racism can persist not just through the isolated actions of racist individuals but at the social level. As the next chapter will show, these are not the only two areas of life where this unfortunate observation can be made.

Questions for Reflection and Discussion

1. What have you previously heard about the challenges of systemic racism (or maybe institutional or structural racism) in policing and housing? To what extent have you identified a social or structural dimension to the problems of the racially disproportionate use of force by police or residential segregation before?

2. How would you evaluate the claim that the objective reasonableness standard functions as a racist form of structural sin by facilitating greater use of force against people of color, especially Black men? What kinds of remedies do you think would be most effective for shifting the restrictions, enablements, and incentives built into the relational connections linking police officers with those whom they police?

3. How would you characterize the link between the historical practice of redlining and the dramatic degree of residential segregation that persists today? Are there restrictions, enablements, and incentives beyond zoning laws that you would say are contributing to the problem?

CHAPTER SIX

Healthcare and Education

The observation that racial disparities exist in health and educational outcomes in the United States is no longer a novel one. The COVID-19 pandemic gave the whole country a first-hand view of the different experiences of healthcare by race in the United States. Early in the pandemic, when we had the fewest resources and the least expertise to help people who came down with COVID, infection rates for Blacks were more than twice the rate for Whites, while Latinos and Native Americans had rates that were more than four times as high as the rate for Whites. Such trends put these individuals in a precarious place, resulting in a consistent racial disparity in COVID death rates throughout the pandemic (when controlling for the different age demographics of each racial group).[1] These data provide just one immediate reminder of the fact that health outcomes vary considerably by racial groups.

Similarly, educational outcomes reflect notable racial disparities too. Overall, roughly 38 percent of the U.S. population had at least a bachelor's degree in 2021. While this included nearly 42 percent of the non-Hispanic White population and over 60 percent of the Asian population, it reflected only 28 percent of the Black population and just under 21 percent of the Hispanic population.[2] Race has a way of impacting education just as much as it does healthcare.

The natural question prompted by these statistics is why. After all, there could be a host of benign explanations for racial differences in healthcare outcomes and educational attainment that have nothing to do with racism. As the national debate about equality of outcome versus equality of opportunity has highlighted, the mere existence of differential outcomes is not taken to be proof of the persistence of racism in our public discourse. One might recognize these disparities and still reject the idea that any form of racial discrimination could be involved.

Given the Catholic understanding of the multifaceted nature of racism as a sinful phenomenon with both personal and social dimensions, Catholics cannot be satisfied with a quick dismissal of unequal outcomes in this manner. Instead, their commitment to the common good as "the good of all and of each individual" (again, the definition St. John Paul II gives in *Sollicitudo Rei Socialis*, no. 38) must prompt them to examine the root causes of these inequities to see if there are ways to better promote the flourishing of all. Part of that process entails asking whether the unequal outcomes stem from unequal opportunities, a question that the category of structural sin helps to disentangle. To that end, this chapter examines healthcare and education and identifies structures of sin that perpetuate racism in these two areas of life, adding to the analysis of policing and housing in the last chapter.

Racism and Structures of Sin in Healthcare

The COVID-19 disparities described above point to two distinct kinds of structural inequalities that affect healthcare outcomes. One kind is not directly tied to healthcare but nonetheless has a profound impact on health. In this sphere, the structural inequalities reflect the "social determinants of health." These are things like the place a person lives, the social connections of one's family of origin, the access to healthy foods, and the other supports of daily life that affect one's risk factors for numerous medical conditions and shape one's ability to get treatments (and to comply with those treatments) when health issues do arise. By one measure, these social determinants account for 80 percent or more of health outcomes, whereas direct medical care is responsible for only 20 percent.[3]

Notably, the social determinants of health are not unaffected by larger racial disparities. Residential segregation means that place is not merely a generic social determinant of health but a profoundly racialized one, too, at least in the United States, because (as we saw in chapter 5) race is a major factor in where people live. The COVID disparities certainly reflected an extended impact of this residential segregation, but this was not the only social determinant involved. The differences at the beginning of the pandemic were also due to the racial sorting of occupations, which meant that White individuals were more likely than their Black, Latino, and Native American peers to have the kinds of jobs that seamlessly shifted online during the 2020 lockdowns. Black, Latino, and Native American workers were more likely to be employed in the "essential" service industries, like in grocery stores, where they were on the front lines without any protective equipment. Work was, therefore, another contributor to the disparities, yet work is likewise influenced by other, interrelated, structural forces, including housing, access to transit, educational opportunities, social capital for securing job interviews, and more. Each of these forces has racial dimensions, too, meaning that the social determinants of health often interact to have a compounding effect.

The Catholic account of structural sin helps us appreciate that these social determinants are not randomly distributed in a neutral manner but are instead heavily influenced by structural factors. The analysis of housing in the last chapter, for instance, reveals that there are and have historically been profound incentives, for some, and restrictions, for others, that have shaped who ends up in the healthiest neighborhoods. As people have followed these incentives or succumbed to their restrictions, the physical landscape of our cities has changed. This has created new incentives for supermarkets to pull out of urban areas and invest more heavily in suburban ones, for shoppers in suburban neighborhoods now have statistically higher incomes, and the new reliance on high-way transportation has made restocking suburban stores easier than urban ones. The result of these structural forces has been an increasing concentration of "food deserts," or neighborhoods without direct access to healthy food markets, among "low-income communities and communities of color."[4] Unsurprisingly, this has negatively affected health in these communities; access to healthy foods is recognized as a significant social determinant of health.

Food is just one example, but it is illustrative of the larger point that both the medical idea of the social determinants of health and the theological concept of structural sin are designed to show. Negative outcomes are not always the result of poor choices made by individuals; often, they are the result of structures that leave some individuals with few options, prompting them to accept unideal outcomes. The social determinants of health are a prime example of these structural forces, representing a structure of sin that supports racial inequalities in healthcare. They are, however, only one-half of the problem, for there are also structures of sin in the provision of medical care itself that contribute to racially disparate health outcomes.

Among the series of restrictions, enablements, and incentives determining access to healthcare in the United States, the most literally structural is the geographic distribution of primary care facilities. According to public health researchers, "racial minorities are more likely to live in primary care shortage areas" than their White counterparts, and they thus rely more heavily on hospitals, especially emergency rooms, for routine medical care.[5] This has a significant effect on health outcomes, as a host of chronic conditions and serious diseases are much more treatable when diagnosed as soon as possible. Thus, disparities in access to primary care can help to explain why Black women are significantly more likely to be diagnosed with breast cancer at later stages than White women and, as a result, have significantly higher mortality rates.[6] Individual structures of sin, meanwhile, influence these disparities in access.

One important set of incentives arises from the health insurance system in the United States. Physicians and primary care practices need money to function, so they logically gravitate toward the areas that can ensure the most reliable payments for the services they provide. Doctors and healthcare systems therefore have an incentive to prioritize areas with more affluent patients because the people with the highest paying jobs have the best health insurance. Indeed, the fact that we have tied health insurance so closely to employment means that doctors will have the least incentive to build their practices in areas with high unemployment or where residents primarily have low-wage jobs. This incentive has racial implications, as "many racial and ethnic minority workers are employed in low-wage jobs that do not provide adequate health insurance," leaving Blacks and Latinos, in particular, uninsured at 1.5 to 2.5 times the rate of Whites.[7] The system linking insurance to employment thus provides an enablement for White workers to access care, whereas it tends to introduce a restriction on racial and ethnic minority workers' access. Our current insurance system, then, functions as a structural sin that encourages racially discriminatory outcomes. Like the social determinants of health, it is another practical illustration of the social dimensions of racism that the U.S. Catholic bishops condemn.

The Catholic understanding of structural sin thus helps to demonstrate that racially disparate health outcomes in the United States are not the happenstance result of individual choices or insignificant anomalies but are, rather, the reflection of racial inequities with deeply structural roots. Importantly, this analysis has also shown that many of these structural roots are interrelated, and this fact makes it all the more essential to explore a fourth sphere of racial inequality with the eyes of faith, as education touches directly on so many of these interrelated forces.

Racism and Structures of Sin in Education

Education, as virtually any economist will insist, is the key that unlocks a host of social and economic opportunities, so it should not be surprising that racial disparities in education play a prominent role in many of the unequal outcomes already discussed. For instance, disparities in the attainment of a college degree are especially relevant for access to healthcare, as workers with a bachelor's degree earn almost double what workers with a high school diploma earn over their lifetimes (an extra $1.2 million, or about an additional $30,000 per year).[8] This earning power translates into greater access to health insurance, among other goods. It therefore matters that attaining a bachelor's degree varies so much by racial and ethnic background.

In the realm of education, there are two significant sets of restrictions, enablements, and incentives that contribute to racial disparities in college completion rates. The first is the uneven educational opportunity available to different racial groups. Because public schooling is a local responsibility, the housing segregation described in the last chapter translates to heavily segregated schools in most parts of the country. The funding structure for local schools, meanwhile, amplifies this segregation and adds a layer of resource inequality. Most states fund public education through a mix of state and local taxes, with local property taxes accounting for significant variations between communities. Districts in wealthier communities have higher property values—typically because they have benefited from redlining—and thus have a better tax base. In contrast, districts in poorer municipalities—often the ones that were redlined—not only have fewer resources because of their smaller tax bases but also fare worse on a relative scale as their wealthier neighbors spend lavishly, creating an educational arms race that pulls families with resources out of poorer districts in search of "better" schools.

The funding structure for public education thus creates a zero-sum game in which neighboring districts compete with one another for teachers and tax bases. The competition, in turn, creates significant incentives for wealthier families to use their economic resources to move to the districts with the best schools, draining the less successful districts of the very resources that could help them compete. Given the structures of sin reinforcing residential segregation, this system primarily benefits the White families who have had more access to intergenerational wealth from home equity. Black, Latino, Native American, and (to a lesser, though not insignificant, extent) Asian families are the primary ones left behind. In urban environments in particular, the funding structures that keep local property taxes local thereby simultaneously become a restriction for these families and an enablement for White families, exacerbating educational inequalities. If funds were balanced at the state level (as some states currently do), there would be a much more equitable distribution of resources among districts, minimizing the arms race and removing the incentives that currently encourage wealthier families to abandon certain districts altogether.

One can easily imagine how these disparities in educational opportunities impact students' opportunities to get into college. Although resources are not the only thing that matters, they certainly make it easier for students to succeed, and, unsurprisingly, wealthier schools send more students to college than poorer ones even when controlling for other demographic variables.[9] The funding system for public education is thus a structural constraint that contributes to inequalities in access to a college education, serving as one mechanism that promotes and preserves racial disparities in education.

Getting to college is not the only hurdle shaping the racial disparities in educational attainment, however. There are also structural enablements on campuses that disproportionately benefit White students. The clearest example is what scholars have described as the "hidden curriculum," or "the set of tacit rules in a formal educational context that insiders consider to be natural and universal."[10] These are things like the fact that "office hours" are the time when a student can stop by a professor's office to ask questions about the class and the hidden knowledge that using this time to introduce oneself to a professor can have a profound impact on one's performance in the course. While seemingly obvious for anyone who has been to office hours before, these "facts" are mystifying for someone who has little familiarity with the standard practices of college campuses and no familiarity with the term "office hours." In recent years, education researchers have underscored the ways this hidden curriculum serves to divide first-generation college students, who are the first in their family to attend a four-year college or university, from their peers whose parents attended college. The latter often have an informal introduction to the hidden curriculum before they arrive on campus, while the former typically must figure out the hidden curriculum on their own.

As a major structural force shaping college success, the hidden curriculum creates an enablement for those who have the luxury of not even noticing that the curriculum is hidden and imposes a restriction on those who do not know what questions to ask to uncover the curriculum that lurks below the surface. Given that first-generation students "are largely from lower-income families and more likely to be minority students than the entire student body," this structural sin has profound implications for the current racial disparities in the attainment of college degrees.[11] Certainly, not all minority students are first-generation students (and vice versa), but the statistical trends mean that the hidden curriculum is a restriction for minority students much more often than it is for their White classmates, and it is an enablement for White students far more often than it is for their Black, Hispanic, Native American, and Asian peers. Insofar as it serves to benefit one racial group at the expense of the flourishing of others, it is rightly condemned as a structure of sin contributing to the social dimensions of racism.

Conclusion

As both this chapter and the previous one have shown, the restrictions, enablements, and incentives that form the basis of sinful social structures are not hard to find in the areas where we see some of the most dramatic racial disparities today. In policing and housing, the law has represented an important structural force facilitating racially discriminatory outcomes. In healthcare and education, the conventional practices of these fields have been the prominent culprits. Whether the issues arise from the law or convention, however, these structural forces represent structures of sin that undermine the flourishing of all. Indicting them with this theological terminology generates two important consequences.

First, the Catholic vision of the relationship between structural sin and personal agency underscores the fact that none of these structures are deterministic. The simple fact that a structure makes racially discriminatory outcomes easier to achieve and thus more likely to occur does not mean that every White person will benefit from them nor that every person of color will be harmed by them. For instance, some Whites will resist the problematic incentives these structures propose to them and pursue more equitable outcomes; others will find that their White racial identity does not completely protect them from the harm of these structures, particularly if they have fewer economic privileges or other marginalized identities. Blacks, Latinos, Asians, and Native Americans will continue to fight against the structural constraints they face and find ways to achieve better outcomes for themselves and their families despite the odds. The Catholic understanding of structural sin suggests that, far from disproving the existence of structures of sin behind the social dimensions of racism today, these kinds of "incongruous outcomes" are a reminder of the ways we preserve our free will and, for that reason, are an added reason to fight more strongly against these structural forces to make them even less deterministic.

Second, the Catholic understanding of structural sin as a form of *sin* reminds us of the importance of taking action to correct the structures of sin that are preserving racism and threatening the common good. Precisely because sin ruptures our relationship with God, it is exactly the kind of thing we should seek to eradicate wherever we encounter it. The final section of the book, therefore, turns to this responsibility, exploring some practical ways Catholics can embrace their call to "a genuine conversion of heart . . . and the reform of our institutions and society" (*Open Wide Our Hearts*, 7).

Questions for Reflection and Discussion

1. How do you evaluate equality of opportunity and equality of outcome? What is your reaction to the chapter's suggestion that Catholics must be concerned about inequalities in outcome when they represent a threat to what St. John Paul II described as "the good of all and of each individual" (*Sollicitudo Rei Socialis*, no. 38)?

2. When you think about your own health, what structural restrictions, enablements, or incentives have influenced your outcomes—for better or worse? Where can you identify "social determinants" affecting your health?

3. Does the funding structure for public schooling in your state do more to promote equality or reinforce inequality between districts? At the college level, are the people of your parish or community more likely to encounter the "hidden curriculum" as an enablement or a restriction? How could the network of your parish or community make the curriculum less hidden?

PART IV

Confronting Racism with Catholic Social Teaching

This final part explores the twofold process of personal conversion and structural transformation that the U.S. Catholic bishops identify as the most appropriate Catholic response to racism. The necessity of both is evident when we recognize that structures of sin contribute to the persistence of racism. Personal conversion is necessary so that individual moral agents can be formed to resist the perverse incentives of sinful social structures and continue to choose to act rightly. Structural change, meanwhile, is essential so that fewer people will have to rely on heroic levels of virtue to do the right thing. As the Servant of God Dorothy Day remarked, "We must try to make that kind of a society in which it is easier for people to be good."[1]

Drawing on what the Vatican describes as "the permanent principles of the Church's social doctrine" (*Compendium of the Social Doctrine of the Church*, no. 160), the two chapters in this part tackle this challenge. Chapter 7 develops a Catholic response to racism grounded in human dignity and the common good, while chapter 8 extends this analysis with an application of solidarity and subsidiarity. The result is a vision for concrete practices Catholics can undertake to confront racial injustice with the eyes of their faith.

CHAPTER SEVEN

Confronting Racism with Human
Dignity and the Common Good

The U.S. Catholic bishops describe Catholic social teaching (CST) as "a rich treasure of wisdom about building a just society and living lives of holiness amidst the challenges of modern society."[1] CST is thus a prime resource for crafting a distinctly Catholic response to the challenges of racism because the twofold tasks of personal conversion and structural change are fundamentally about living lives of holiness in this fallen world and striving to build a more just society in the meantime. By its very nature, CST orients Catholics toward more holistic solutions to the challenges of modern society.

The application of CST to a concrete problem often requires a bit of translation, however. To help with this process, the Vatican's Pontifical Council for Justice and Peace has identified four "permanent principles" of CST that are to serve as "the primary and fundamental perameters [*sic*] of reference for interpreting and evaluating social phenomena" (*Compendium of the Social Doctrine of the Church*, no. 161). Consistent with this vision, part IV uses the four permanent principles of CST to discuss an effective Catholic response to racism, beginning with the principles of human dignity and the common good.

81

The Principle of Human Dignity

Arguably no principle is more central to CST or more pertinent to the issue of racism than that of human dignity. The *Compendium* identifies human dignity as "the foundation of all the other principles and content of the Church's social doctrine" (no. 160), highlighting its centrality. Meanwhile, the U.S. Catholic bishops consistently maintain that racism "violat[es] the dignity inherent in each person" (*Open Wide Our Hearts*, 30), revealing that a restoration of dignity must be at the heart of the personal conversion and structural change required to transcend racism.

While the idea of embracing human dignity hopefully sounds like a no-brainer, the Catholic understanding of what this principle means in practice sets a high bar, because it demands a much more radical commitment to *all* of one's neighbors than most of us are ready to accept. The easiest way to see the weight of this responsibility is to contrast the robust notion of human dignity found in CST with the fickler definition that circulates in today's U.S. culture.

As Catholic moral theologian Kelly Johnson points out, the Catholic account asserts that "the dignity of the person is not something we achieve ourselves or give to one another—it is intrinsic in a person's creation by the Father of Jesus."[2] This is in stark contrast to the prevailing U.S. ethos that idolizes a particular brand of individualism and stresses that one's value must be earned. Although we do not typically think of this as a matter of "dignity," the truth is that this conventional perspective suggests there are some people who do not deserve society's care and attention because they have not yet done enough to prove that they are worth our resources. The principle of human dignity found in CST is much more encompassing, underscoring the "love of the actual persons who are God's family, even when those persons don't fit into political programs or even when they complicate received theological notions."[3] There is not a single person outside the principle of human dignity in the Catholic account.

How, then, might the principle of human dignity shape a Catholic response to racism? At the level of personal conversion, the Catholic conception of human dignity provides an important buffer against the problematic influences of the sinful social structures that currently work to reinforce cultural racism. After all, one part of that cultural racism is the set of damaging assumptions, like the elision of Black men with danger, that encourages us to look past the humanity of our neighbors and see them as abstract "threats." When we embrace the Catholic assumption that dignity is not something one earns but rather something everyone is gifted by virtue of their existence as human beings made in the image and likeness of God, we can resist these stereotypical reductionisms and better form our consciences—and the moral intuitions influencing our practical judgments—to be in line with our theological convictions.

One way to embody this acceptance of the Catholic principle of human dignity is to actively interrogate our reaction anytime broader cultural assumptions try to tell us someone is not worthy of dignity so that we counter it with a reaffirmation of the inherent dignity of all. To give an example from relatively recent events, consider what happened in early 2022 when the United States faced a shortage of baby formula and pictures circulated online of well-stocked shelves at U.S. border processing centers, where federal supplies for detained immigrants included an ample stock of baby formula. The juxtaposition was not meant to call attention to the shortage in general, nor was it meant to encourage improved access for all; instead, the public narrative was designed to stoke outrage at the fact that migrants were getting fed while the babies of American citizens struggled to eat. The implicit message was that the former should not be getting food at all, or at least not until every "American" baby had had their fill. The desired reaction only makes sense, however, if one accepts that there is a drastic difference in "worthiness" by citizenship status. The Catholic account of human dignity highlights the falsity of this vision and reminds us that all these babies deserve to be fed.

If we can reject the false dichotomies found in these and other cultural narratives and can affirm the inherent dignity of those who seem so "unworthy" by our collective social standards, then we can limit the influence of these social ideals on our moral intuitions and thus make it easier for our consciences to affirm the Catholic conviction that human dignity never has to be proven or earned. In this way, we will counter the power of those structures of sin that help racism persist. We can, with God's help, realize precisely what the U.S. Catholic bishops pray will come to pass—namely, "that prejudice and animosity will no longer infect our minds or hearts but will be replaced with a love that respects the dignity of each person" (*Open Wide Our Hearts*, 32).

Significantly, this vision of human dignity should also impact the pursuit of structural transformation. In the sphere of policing, for instance, a commitment to the equal inherent dignity of both police officers and those whom they police should prompt us to advocate for a legal structure that accounts for the value of every life when interactions turn violent. Although the current objective reasonableness standard presumably intends to do this, as we saw in chapter 5, that is not how the legal structure operates in practice since it functionally gives the benefit of the doubt primarily to one side in these incidents. Something like the substantive due process standard, meanwhile, would encourage an analysis built around a more equal footing.

Likewise, in the realm of housing, a recognition of the inherent dignity of all would militate against the "NIMBYism" (the attitude that some things a community might need should go somewhere else and "Not In My Back Yard") that pressures municipalities—especially the wealthier, and Whiter, suburban ones—to fight against zoning changes that would make it easier for renters to enter a community. When we stress that dignity is not earned by securing a mortgage but rather honored when basic needs like housing are met, the rationales for opposing changes in our neighborhoods look far less compelling. As a result, avenues for greater racial diversity in housing open, countering the structural sins still perpetuating residential segregation.

Of course, as these examples illustrate, the principle of human dignity is closely aligned with other principles in CST, most evidently the principle of the common good, because acknowledging my neighbor's equal right to the goods I enjoy is a logical precondition for a commitment to "the good of all and of each individual" (*Sollicitudo Rei Socialis*, no. 38). This kind of interconnection is a feature of the permanent principles in CST, which "must be appreciated in their unity, interrelatedness and articulation" (*Compendium of the Social Doctrine of the Church*, no. 162). In keeping with this vision, then, I want to discuss how the principle of the common good can complement the practices that the principle of human dignity identifies in a Catholic response to racism.

The Principle of the Common Good

Throughout this book I have appealed, as I just did, to St. John Paul II's definition of the common good as "the good of all and of each individual." This is an essential description for CST because it keeps the collective concerns of the common good in direct contact with the personalist emphases of the principle of human dignity. It is not enough, from the Catholic perspective, to maximize the greatest good for the greatest number of people if some individuals are left behind so that the majority can prosper. This is the point of stressing the good of all *and* of each individual. Given the ways that racism often pits a racial majority against members of minoritized racial groups, one can quickly see how important this multipart definition will be for an adequate Catholic response to racism.

How do we realize the good of all and of each individual? First, we can recall the Second Vatican Council's presentation of the common good as "the sum total of social conditions which allow people, either as groups or as individuals, to reach their fulfillment more fully and more easily." This definition gives further content to our responsibility to honor human dignity, inviting us to consider "all that is necessary for living a genuinely human life: for example, food, clothing, housing, the right freely to choose their state of life and set up a family, the right to education, work, to their good name, to respect" (*Gaudium et Spes*, no. 26). These concrete considerations are especially pertinent for responding to racism, where structures of sin affect the distribution of these goods in ways that, as this book has shown, often involve and exacerbate racial inequalities.

Second, we can rely on the U.S. Catholic bishops, who have closely connected the common good to justice and insist that the common good is only fully realized when all members of the community have an opportunity to play a part in the specification and realization of their community's common good (*Economic Justice for All*, no. 85).[4] "Persons have an obligation to be active and productive participants in the life of society," the bishops explain, and "society has a duty to enable them to participate in this way" (no. 71). Much like the Second Vatican Council's vision, this emphasis on expanding access and participation highlights the relevance of the common good in the Catholic response to racism, for the structures of sin that help racism persist often have the effect of restricting participation in community life.

In terms of shaping a response to racism, then, the principle of the common good asks each of us to remember that the good of all and of each individual is only served when it is possible for "*all* persons to share in and contribute to the common good" (*Economic Justice for All*, no. 88, emphasis in original). At the personal level, the principle therefore equips us to better identify the perverse incentives and unequal restrictions that structures of sin hide so effectively, because an orientation to the common good constantly prods us to assess who is able to join us in our common projects and who is regularly excluded. Shocking us from complacency and denial, this permanent principle shines a light on the structural barriers that are often invisible to those of us who have the luxury of skating by without running into them but that are so impactful to those whose race or social situation makes them unavoidable.

The hidden curriculum described in the case of education offers a prime example of the shift in perspective the common good entails. For those who are familiar with the everyday routines of college life, the hidden curriculum is rarely seen as an obstacle because they know how to get around it and, in fact, benefit from it. For a first-generation student, however, the hidden curriculum is a direct barrier to college success, closing doors that are left open to others. By turning our attention to the question of access, the principle of the common good invites us to interrogate the hidden curriculum and, naturally, encourages us to take the necessary action to remove this unequal barrier to access. In this way, the principle prompts personal conversion by empowering us to see the world with new eyes and then orients that conversion to structural change, spurring us to dismantle the structural obstacles we discover with our renewed vision.

The principle of the common good invites a similar recognition when applied to healthcare. As chapter 6 of this book discussed, the fundamental structural constraint in healthcare is one of access, as the reliance on employment for health insurance affects both access to affordable healthcare and the geographic distribution of primary care offices in a manner heavily influenced by race. By emphasizing healthcare as one of the conditions of the social life to which Catholics must attend, the principle of the common good helps us recognize an injustice that threatens the well-being of Black, Hispanic, Native American, and Asian families and undermines their ability to participate in and contribute to the life of our communities. It also encourages us to advocate for structural changes that would expand access to affordable health care, say, by uncoupling health insurance and employment in pursuit of the U.S. Catholic bishops' "commit[ment] to the ideals of universal and affordable health care" for all.[5]

These are, of course, but two illustrations of the ways Catholics can incorporate the principle of the common good in their response to the multifaceted problem of racism. The principle could similarly extend to policing and housing as well as other areas where the unacceptable incentives, enablements, and restrictions of structural sins continue to promote racist attitudes and yield racially discriminatory results. In all these cases, the principle of the common good has the potential to clarify our vision and inspire our resolve so that we can better identify and correct the structural injustices that allow racism, at both the personal and social levels, to persist.

Conclusion

This brief discussion of the principles of human dignity and the common good is admittedly incomplete. Certainly, the application of these principles has been far from comprehensive. This is not inherently a problem, however, as long as the examples in this chapter can be seen as illustrative rather than exhaustive. The point, then, is not to articulate all the solutions, as though there was only one possible answer to each of the structures of sin that facilitate racial inequalities today. Instead, the aim (as in all of part IV) is to establish the resources Catholics can use to arrive at these solutions. Consequently, the partial illustrations of this chapter can serve to facilitate rather than frustrate the development of a Catholic response to racism, provided that the process of challenging messages of unworthiness and interrogating access continues in applications to other areas where racial discrimination continues. The chapter thus lays a solid foundation for a Catholic response to racism. Given the Vatican's emphasis on the essential unity of the four permanent principles of CST, however, we must continue to build on that foundation with a consideration of what the principles of solidarity and subsidiarity can add to the conversation.

Questions for Reflection and Discussion

1. How do you react to the contrast between the Catholic conception of human dignity as an inherent feature of every human

person and the more common connection between worthiness and individual productivity that the chapter suggests is prevalent in U.S. society? To what extent do you recognize this tension in your own experience?

2. Which of the three descriptions of the common good appeals to you most? Why do you gravitate to this one rather than the others? How does your preferred understanding of the common good impact the solutions to the challenges of education and healthcare described in this chapter?

3. The chapter applies the principle of human dignity to the questions of policing and housing and the principle of the common good to education and healthcare. What would it look like to extend each principle to the other two areas? What would it look like to apply each principle to other realms where you have seen racial inequalities?

CHAPTER EIGHT

Confronting Racism with Solidarity and Subsidiarity

While all four permanent principles of CST are necessarily linked, the final two principles of solidarity and subsidiarity are especially tightly connected. "The principle of subsidiarity must remain closely linked to the principle of solidarity and vice versa," Pope Benedict XVI insists in his 2009 social encyclical, *Caritas in Veritate*, because "the former without the latter gives way to social privatism, while the latter without the former gives way to paternalist social assistance that is demeaning to those in need" (no. 58).[1] Apart, subsidiarity and solidarity each point us toward dangerous extremes, either by reducing our social responsibilities to a libertarian spirit of "live and let live" that undermines the Catholic vision of the social nature of the human person (in the case of subsidiarity), or by insisting on top-down solutions to shared problems that fail to account for personal freedom and local variation (in the case of solidarity). When combined, however, subsidiarity and solidarity yield effective proposals for orienting social life to the protection of human dignity and the promotion of the common good.

With respect to racism, these two principles add to the insights distilled from the principles of human dignity and the common good discussed in the last chapter. Solidarity can help strengthen our resolve to expand access to our shared community, as the

common good would demand, even when this call imposes noticeable costs on us. Subsidiarity, meanwhile, reminds us that the
analysis of structural obstacles cannot be confined to one sphere
of our social life alone but must also extend to our intermediary
organizations and institutions, including those closest to home.
Together with the principles of human dignity and the common
good, they yield a richly Catholic response to racism.

The Principle of Solidarity

Catholic theologians talk about solidarity having both a descriptive and a prescriptive element. Descriptively, solidarity captures
the fact that all human beings are connected by virtue of both our
shared creation in the image and likeness of God and our common
destiny as creatures redeemed through the mystery of the incarna-
tion, in which Christ took on the same humanity that unites us
now. Prescriptively, solidarity indicates that we have ethical obligations as a result of the fact that we are innately connected to all
other members of the human race. As St. John Paul II explained,
solidarity allows us to realize that "we are all really responsible for
all" and should act accordingly (*Sollicitudo Rei Socialis*, no. 38).

The challenge, of course, is to figure out exactly what it means
to act accordingly once we have accepted that we are members of
the same human family, regardless of any racial or ethnic divisions
that our social contexts might present to us. Pope Francis argues
that acting in accordance with this descriptive fact of our shared
humanity demands "something more than a few sporadic acts of
generosity. It presumes the creation of a new mindset which thinks
in terms of community and the priority of the life of all over the
appropriation of goods by a few" (*Evangelii Gaudium*, no. 188).
As David Cloutier explains, this makes solidarity the opposite of
competition, at least competition in the "sense that I have to get
some [particular] good before someone else does."[2] Whereas this
kind of competition encourages people to prioritize their self-
interest, the "new mindset" of solidarity asks us to think about

what is good for the life of our community first. Just as important, it simultaneously expands our vision of that community so it is no longer confined to a narrow subset of the true human family, like our immediate blood relatives or our own racial groups.

Solidarity's new mindset presents a tension with the way we are trained to think about social responsibilities in the United States. I remember having a conversation with a neighbor shortly after we moved to Wisconsin. We were both watching our children play, and she expressed a fairly typical set of parental anxieties about what the future might look like for her kids. I was particularly struck by how she characterized the challenges ahead. Lamenting the rise in economic inequality and the increasingly limited supply of "good paying" jobs, this woman said she was living in this suburban community, with its highly rated schools, because she wanted to make sure that her children would grow up to become one of the few who would make it to the top.

By conventional U.S. standards, my neighbor's reaction was perfectly logical. If there are only going to be so many opportunities to succeed, why would a mother not pour all her energy into guiding her own children to one of the dwindling opportunities that remain? By the logic of solidarity, however, this woman's reaction was tragic because it simply accepted a dramatic split between winners and losers as a societal fact of life and found nothing objectionable about that division as long as her kids were the winners and the losers were someone else's kids. A genuine embrace of the descriptive fact of solidarity would reject complacency in the face of this winners-and-losers dichotomy and encourage any parent who recognized it to pour his or her energy into challenging the inequality itself so that all God's children might succeed and not just the ones who are biologically (or legally) connected to us.

In order to make this attitude a reality, solidarity requires a newfound willingness to accept individual burdens for the sake of collective benefits. As St. John Paul II insisted, solidarity calls us to a radical love of neighbor. Our neighbor is to be loved "with the same love with which the Lord loves him or her; and for that person's sake one must be ready for sacrifice, even the ultimate one: to lay down one's life for the brethren" (*Sollicitudo Rei Socialis*, no. 40). The principle of solidarity means that we should be prepared to lose something so that our neighbors, particularly those who are poor and on the margins, can have what they need to survive.

This openness to sacrifice is especially relevant in the Catholic response to racism, for the perverse incentives and unequal restrictions of racially discriminatory structures of sin pit self-interest against racial justice. Thus, zoning laws successfully perpetuate residential segregation because current property owners fear that new multifamily developments will lower their property values. Similarly, school funding structures preserve educational inequalities by keeping local money within the confines of the district because families do not want to see "their" money going to fund "other" schools. And so on.

The principle of solidarity interrupts this logic, inspiring Catholics to accept that the well-being of all might require sacrifices from some, particularly the most well off. As Cloutier's evaluation of the practice of solidarity notes, restrictive zoning laws have made homes in wealthier neighborhoods with the strongest schools a "positional good" whose value stems from its higher position relative to homes in other districts with worse-performing schools. In this arrangement, any change to zoning laws that would expand the supply of housing would (as a matter of basic economics) lower the cost of housing throughout the community, reducing property values for existing homeowners. "The call to solidarity means, however, that these [Catholic] families can certainly support such efforts and can at least avoid opposing efforts that they might perceive as hurting them."[3] They can, in other words, accept the hit to their property values that a restoration of racial equality in access to housing and education will almost certainly entail because solidarity will allow them to see that this is a good burden to bear for the sake of one's neighbor.

If Catholics consistently adopt this willingness to sacrifice at least some of their own self-interest for the well-being of others, they will showcase the solidarity that St. John Paul II described as "not a feeling of vague compassion or shallow distress at the misfortunes of so many people, both near and far . . . [but] a firm and persevering determination to commit oneself to the common good" (*Sollicitudo Rei Socialis*, no. 38). They will therefore have the necessary disposition to challenge the structures of sin that encourage White communities to see more inclusive zoning laws and more diverse neighborhoods as a threat to their financial stability because they will recognize that some goods are more important than economic returns. While there are multiple ways Catholics can be encouraged to make these shifts and adopt this new mindset of solidarity, one of the most helpful mechanisms revolves around the final permanent principle: subsidiarity.

The Principle of Subsidiarity

Subsidiarity is a peculiarly Catholic principle that emphasizes the dignity of the human person as a creature endowed with free will who is simultaneously social in nature. Much like solidarity, this principle has two interrelated functions. On one hand, subsidiarity has a restraining function that creates the space for small-scale associations to flourish so that more people can realize their social nature. On the other hand, subsidiarity has an obliging function that imposes a responsibility on larger-scale organizations to provide the resources smaller-scale associations need to flourish. The easiest way to understand both functions is to think about the Girl Scout Cookie Program.

In the United States, the Girl Scouts is a massive national organization composed of thousands of smaller-scale constituent parts known as troops. Every year the local troops cooperate with the national organization to bring hundreds of millions of boxes of cookies to hungry customers. To do this effectively, they rely on the principle of subsidiarity (otherwise known as the reason my wife and I become a mini movie production company each spring as we work with our daughter to design, film, and edit advertising videos for her personal cookie sales). First, local troops have the flexibility to determine how many cookies they are going to sell and to decide what they want to do with the money they raise. This gives the girls immediate ownership over the process, making them more engaged in the cookie campaign and, more importantly, teaching them lifelong skills about how to collaboratively set goals and achieve them. The national organization gives troops this freedom in a manner that is consistent with the restraining function of subsidiarity, because Girl Scouts USA refuses to tell the troops what to do at the granular level.

The Girl Scout Cookie Program also reflects the obliging function of subsidiarity because the national organization does not simply leave local troops to figure everything out on their own. Instead, Girl Scouts USA provides a host of resources to local councils, service units, and troops to allow the girls to fulfill their cookie orders. Rather than telling every troop to contract with a local bakery, for instance, Girl Scouts USA has a massive agreement with two bakeries and works with the local councils to get the cookies from these bakeries to the troops.

The Girl Scout Cookie Program thus represents the two sides of the principle of subsidiarity, which the moral theologian Meghan Clark summarized as the conviction that "decisions should be made *at the lowest level possible and the highest level necessary*."[4] The national organization adopts the restraining function of subsidiarity and respects the rights of the local troops to make their own choices about the decisions that affect them directly (lowest level possible). At the same time, the national organization also follows subsidiarity's obliging function to create the structures that allow the troops to implement these decisions (highest level necessary). As a result, the Girl Scout Cookie Program gives more girls more meaningful involvement in the enterprise, affirming their free will by deferring to local judgments while also allowing them to connect with others and contribute to something bigger than themselves through the institutional supports of the national organization's structure.

To put these benefits in more theological terms, the principle of subsidiarity stresses the importance of small-scale social connections because this is the place where everyone can answer their call to contribute to the common good. If the Girl Scout Cookie Program were run entirely at the national level, there would be far fewer girls actively involved in decision-making, so most scouts would make limited contributions to the common good. By supporting local autonomy, however, the Girl Scout Cookie Program lets every girl take an active role in the determination of the common good of their troop, empowering each of them to fulfill what CST would describe as a fundamental dimension of their social vocation.

In the realm of racism, subsidiarity's emphasis on the power of the local helps to remind us that any genuine response to the challenges of racism must not neglect "the relationships between individuals and intermediate social groupings, which . . . strengthens the social fabric and constitutes the basis of a true community of persons" (*Compendium of the Social Doctrine of the Church*, no. 185). This is an essential observation, for it underscores that structures—and, thus, structures of sin—emerge from relationships and have their most profound influence as a result of the social pressures they exert. As chapter 4 explained, once these social pressures transform our moral intuitions, they shape our decisions and thus our actions. What is easy to miss, and what the principle of subsidiarity helps us recognize, is that the strongest social pressures are the ones that come from the people closest to us. If we want to correct our moral intuitions and ensure that they affirm the dignity of all races rather than the superiority of some, we need to take heed of the principle of subsidiarity and assess whether we are immersing ourselves in the social groups that are going to help us develop the right affective judgments.

One way to incorporate the principle of subsidiarity into our response to racism, then, is to diversify our immediate social networks. We should strive for a genuine "culture of encounter" that cultivates authentic relationships across the racial divide and supports a network "where differences coexist, complementing, enriching and reciprocally illuminating one another" (*Fratelli Tutti*, no. 215). With such connections in place, we are less likely to fall prey to broad cultural stereotypes about other races, because we can refute these abstract assertions with concrete illustrations from our own encounters, replacing the vague allusions to, say, "Black people" with our own knowledge of the reality of our Black friends. As Fr. Bryan Massingale insists, "deep inter-racial friendship and love can shatter the false personal identity built upon the racialized 'set of meanings and values' that informs American society."[5]

Significantly, this implementation of subsidiarity also invites us into new relationships of solidarity (what Massingale describes as "cross-racial solidarity"[6]), which is perfectly consistent with the close connection between these two principles in CST. Indeed, it is important that we see subsidiarity in contact with solidarity because solidarity is intrinsically ordered to action, and we must choose to act in response to the racial injustices the new friendships of subsidiarity will inevitably uncover for us. When we augment personal conversion with structural change in this way, subsidiarity's two interrelated functions will be especially relevant, as they will help us find solutions that create empowering relationships, not top-down solutions that replicate a "white savior complex."

To give one example, subsidiarity encourages well-intentioned Catholics hoping to address the disparities in healthcare to prioritize input from the communities themselves that need better access rather than trying to transplant the conventional model of healthcare delivery from another neighborhood as though it were a uniform good. This may seem like an obvious strategy, but history shows us that it is not, as local communities' wishes are often overridden by well-meaning organizations that place greater trust in their own experts, subverting the principle of subsidiarity. Subsidiarity helps us appreciate that each community is different and encourages the creation of partnerships rather than "solutions."

Subsidiarity also has one final implication for Catholics looking to respond to the sin of racism. By calling attention to the social connections that are closest to us, subsidiarity also forces us to assess the impact and influence of the church itself, beginning with our local parish. Unfortunately, the geographic nature of most Catholic parishes means that our immediate faith communities often reinforce, rather than reject, the pitfalls of residential segregation, serving to further separate us from the very relationships that can inspire our personal conversion away from cultural forms of racism and empower our project of structural transformation. Just as the Sermon on the Mount informs us that true moral change starts from within, so the principle of subsidiarity asks us to get our own house in order first. This will likely mean outreach opportunities and new partnerships, perhaps even through shared liturgies that can unite racially diverse (and segregated) Catholic parishes. Or, in those areas where racial divisions follow denominations and not just geography, it may mean ecumenical projects. If we take the principle of subsidiarity seriously, though, we will recognize the importance of this work and strive to make our local church the kind of place that reflects the values we want to have forming our consciences and shaping our moral intuitions.

Conclusion

In this chapter, the principle of solidarity and the principle of subsidiarity have been used to provide some additional details about the strategies that can orient the Catholic response to racism toward an affirmation of human dignity and the realization of the common good. Insofar as solidarity expands our understanding of the people for whom we should be willing to sacrifice, it aids in our recognition of the inherent dignity of all human beings and empowers our pursuit of the common good. Meanwhile, to the extent that subsidiarity helps us create the small-scale social affiliations that give more people the opportunity to participate in the life of their community, it expands access to the common good and reinforces the dignity of everyone as a valuable member of our shared social life.

The applications in this chapter highlight not only the interrelated nature of the permanent principles of CST but also the Vatican's assertion that the only way "to understand [the principles] completely" is "to act in accordance with them" (*Compendium of the Social Doctrine of the Church*, no. 163). What this implies is that we should expect to come to a better appreciation of what each of these principles means for the fight against racism as we try to implement them in our own lives. Rather than providing the perfect answer to the pain of racism all at once, these principles are valuable because they offer us the starting point we need to embark on a journey that, much like the kingdom of God that inspires it, will provide *an answer* that is "already" effective but "not yet" the full solution.

Questions for Reflection and Discussion

1. How do you react to the idea that solidarity encourages us to accept individual burdens for the sake of collective benefits? How easy is it for you to embrace this prescriptive element of solidarity?

2. To what extent does subsidiarity's emphasis on the power of smaller-scale associations align with your own experiences? What small-scale organizations would you like to harness in the fight against racism?

3. What connections do you see between the four permanent principles of human dignity, the common good, solidarity, and subsidiarity? How would you like to combine these four principles in your own response to the challenges of racism?

Conclusion

I started this book with some honest reflections on my own experience, and I feel it is appropriate to finish in the same fashion. I want, more specifically, to articulate one hope and two fears I have about this book as it comes to its close.

First, a word about hope. I hope the book has provided some greater clarity about the fact that today's national reckoning with racism is not at odds with the Catholic faith but can become an invitation to a deeper engagement with it. The concept of structural sin, for all its technical peculiarity, gives Catholics every reason to respond to claims about institutional racism or structural racism or systemic racism not with a deep suspicion but instead with a sympathetic ear. Given everything our faith teaches about the damage of sin in our fallen world, why would we suggest that the sin of racism is any different and deny that it could be woven into the fabric of our social life? If anything, the persistence of racism, which Pope Francis has highlighted, suggests that this particular sin is *more* likely to become lodged in that fabric. By emphasizing the powerful enablements, incentives, and restrictions built into the webs that emerge from our relationships, the concept of structural sin gives us the tools to pinpoint the places where racism has in fact burrowed its way into our social life.

Hopefully, then, the book can counteract what is perhaps the most damaging ability of structural sin to operate so seamlessly in society that we rarely notice its causal influence. Much like the provocative ending of the film *The Usual Suspects* points out when one of the characters proclaims, "The greatest trick the devil ever pulled was convincing the world he didn't exist,"[1] the structural nature of structural sins makes each one difficult to uncover, leaving many to conclude that structural sins cannot possibly exist. To the extent that its analyses interrupt a natural tendency toward this denial, this book will serve a valuable purpose.

As much as this hope may be valuable, I still think the greatest insights about the purpose of this book come from two fears (among many) that I have about the text as well. The first fear is my concern that the contents of the book will leave us feeling like we have done enough. You know from the introduction that I am well aware of my shortcomings in the sphere of racial justice, and I mentioned that this book is part of my own struggle with this reality. As I come to the end of the text, I now recognize a new temptation to use the book as proof of my progress. As much as I hope the book has an impact, I also know that ideas in the abstract will not change the status quo. Only ideas that lead to action can yield meaningful results.

I do not intend to downplay the significance of the work that this book invites us to undertake. One popular refrain in response to George Floyd's murder in 2020 was the call for people—especially White people—to "educate themselves" about the realities of racism and their own complicities in it. Coming to a deeper appreciation of the social dimensions of racism through the theological idea of structural sin fits within that project, so it is not as if the book does *nothing*. Nevertheless, this education must be for a purpose, and as the resources of our faith indicate, personal conversion and structural transformation are the two forms this purpose should take in the case of racism. Simply writing this book (or simply reading it) is no substitute for these essential tasks. To be effective, the book must be the start of a journey rather than the rest stop that turns into a dead end.

Recognizing the need to do more, however, prompts my second fear: that this book might have the effect of leaving us feeling like we cannot possibly do enough. To the extent that the book is successful in showcasing the structures of sin behind racial inequalities, it has the effect of revealing the enormity of the challenges ahead of us. The conclusion is that we cannot rid racism simply by removing racists. We must also get to the structures of sin, the perverse incentives and unequal burdens, that generate the dramatic racial disparities we still see today. At that level, change gets even more complicated. As the Adrian Dominican theologian Sr. Jamie Phelps explains, in understated fashion, "Personal change is difficult. Social change is formidable."[2]

Once we truly recognize what is at stake, it is not hard to imagine that we would become paralyzed by the scope and difficulty of the tasks our faith demands. How do I, as one individual, dismantle the structures of sin preserving residential segregation? Redlining lasted for decades and created a wealth gap that has compounded over generations. There seems to be almost nothing one can do about it now. Sadly, one could say the same for all the other illustrations of structural sin that give racism its social influence, from the ones discussed in this book to the ones left unaddressed. There is a real danger, then, that we will acknowledge the problem, feel overwhelmed by its scale, and choose to do nothing about it because we cannot figure out where we would even begin.

The counterpoint to this fear is to arrive at a more honest assessment of two things: what we are actually called to do and what we have to offer in response to that call. With respect to the former, there is no way we would not be overwhelmed if we thought we had to develop a magical solution to all the structures of sin perpetuating racism in this country. No one can achieve something so all-encompassing. As soon as we can accept this insight, though, we can then move on to the narrower question of what we *can* do. As a college friend of mine declared (in what I now realize was a paraphrase of the so-called Romero Prayer written by Bishop Ken Untener), recognizing we cannot do everything frees us to do something.[3]

In the realm of racism, we can experience this freedom whenever we shift our focus from the scale of a problem well beyond our control to the potential of any of the partial solutions that we can control. Thus, for example, supporting a new apartment development in a wealthier suburb will not undo residential segregation, but it might remove a structural obstacle for an individual family, giving us new neighbors who invite new forms of solidarity.

Our efforts to do something will be most effective if they are rooted in the second honest assessment I mentioned, the one about our self-understanding. We all have different gifts, which means that some of us are better suited to certain tasks than others. An essential part of discerning how to respond to the structures of sin supporting racial disparities is, therefore, a careful discernment of the unique set of responses that will allow each of us to use our strengths to pursue the portion of the overall solution that we can address most effectively.

The answer to my fears, then, is a bit of humility. As a virtue, humility strikes the proper balance between thinking too little of ourselves (and underestimating our potential) and thinking too much of ourselves (and failing to attend to the limitations of our capacities). If we can channel both these impulses and truly understand our place in the world, we will not only reject the pride that deceives us into thinking our work is done already, but we will also dismiss the false humility that suggests we have nothing consequential to offer. We will, in other words, finally be free to do something.

Questions for Reflection and Discussion

1. Do you feel the author's hopes for this book have been realized? Do you share either of the fears described in this conclusion? Why or why not?

2. Considering the book as a whole, what aspects were most compelling for you? What portions were most disappointing?

3. What strengths do you see in yourself for the fight against racism? As you move away from the pressure to do everything and focus on the freedom to do something, what areas of action seem most important for your response?

Notes

Introduction

1. John L. Allen Jr., "Francis and the 'Culture of Encounter,'" *NCR Today*, December 20, 2013, https://www.ncronline.org/blogs/ncr-today/francis-and -culture-encounter.

2. Antonio Spadaro, "A Big Heart Open to God: An Interview with Pope Francis," *America*, September 30, 2013, https://www.americamagazine.org /faith/2013/09/30/big-heart-open-god-interview-pope-francis.

3. For one Black Catholic's account of the important role White Catholics need to play in the fight against racism, see Bryan N. Massingale, "The Assumptions of White Privilege and What We Can Do about It," *National Catholic Reporter*, June 1, 2020, https://www.ncronline.org/news/opinion /assumptions-white-privilege-and-what-we-can-do-about-it.

4. Robin DiAngelo, *White Fragility: Why It's So Hard for White People to Talk about Racism* (Boston: Beacon Press, 2018).

5. *Gaudium et Spes*, in Austin Flannery, ed., *Vatican Council II: Constitutions, Decrees, Declarations; The Basic Sixteen Documents* (Collegeville, MN: Liturgical Press, 2014).

6. Thomas Aquinas, *Summa Theologiae*, I-II, q. 8, a. 1, available online at https://www.newadvent.org/summa/2008.htm#article1.

7. Pope Francis, *Evangelii Gaudium* (Rome: Libreria Editrice Vaticana, 2013).

8. Pontifical Council for Justice and Peace, *Compendium of the Social Doctrine of the Church*, available online at https://www.vatican.va/roman _curia/pontifical_councils/justpeace/documents/rc_pc_justpeace_doc _20060526_compendio-dott-soc_en.html.

Chapter 1

1. Pope Francis, General Audience, Library of the Apostolic Palace, June 3, 2020, https://www.vatican.va/content/francesco/en/audiences/2020/documents/papa-francesco_20200603_udienza-generale.html.

2. United States Conference of Catholic Bishops, *Open Wide Our Hearts: The Enduring Call to Love; A Pastoral Letter against Racism* (Washington, DC: United States Conference of Catholic Bishops, 2018), available online at https://www.usccb.org/resources/open-wide-our-hearts_0.pdf.

3. Pope Francis, *Fratelli Tutti* (Rome: Libreria Editrice Vaticana, 2020).

4. Bryan N. Massingale, *Racial Justice and the Catholic Church* (Maryknoll, NY: Orbis Books, 2010), 13.

5. Matthew Impelli, "Student's Online Comment about 'Auctioning off Black Classmates' Sparks Investigation," *Newsweek*, September 15, 2021, https://www.newsweek.com/students-online-comment-about-auctioning-off-black-classmates-sparks-investigation-1629503.

6. Daniel J. Harrington, ed., *The Gospel of Matthew*, Sacra Pagina series (Collegeville, MN: Liturgical Press, 2007), 17.

7. Marilynn B. Brewer, "The Psychology of Prejudice: Ingroup Love or Outgroup Hate?," *Journal of Social Issues* 55, no. 3 (1999): 429–44.

8. National Conference of Catholic Bishops, *Brothers and Sisters to Us: Pastoral Letter on Racism*, 1979, available online at https://www.usccb.org/committees/african-american-affairs/brothers-and-sisters-us.

9. Bryan N. Massingale, "The Assumptions of White Privilege and What We Can Do about It," *National Catholic Reporter*, June 1, 2020, https://www.ncronline.org/news/opinion/assumptions-white-privilege-and-what-we-can-do-about-it.

10. Vernā Myers, "How to Overcome Our Biases? Walk Boldly Toward Them," filmed November 2014 at TEDxBeaconStreet, *TED*, https://www.ted.com/talks/verna_myers_how_to_overcome_our_biases_walk_boldly_toward_them.

11. Massingale, "Assumptions of White Privilege."

Chapter 2

1. Darlene Fozard Weaver, "Taking Sin Seriously," *Journal of Religious Ethics* 31, no. 1 (Spring 2003): 62.

2. John Paul II, *Reconciliatio et Paenitentia*, December 2, 1984, https://www.vatican.va/content/john-paul-ii/en/apost_exhortations/documents/hf_jp-ii_exh_02121984_reconciliatio-et-paenitentia.html.

3. Bryan N. Massingale, "Conscience Formation and the Challenge of Unconscious Racial Bias," in *Conscience and Catholicism: Rights, Responsibilities, and Institutional Responses*, ed. David E. DeCosse and Kristin E. Heyer (Maryknoll, NY: Orbis Books, 2015), 57.

4. Massingale, "Conscience Formation," 57. See also Bryan N. Massingale, *Racial Justice and the Catholic Church* (Maryknoll, NY: Orbis Books, 2010), 24–26.

5. Michael G. Vaughn et al., "Criminal Epidemiology and the Immigrant Paradox: Intergenerational Discontinuity in Violence and Antisocial Behavior among Immigrants," *Journal of Criminal Justice* 42, no. 6 (November–December 2014): 483.

6. Massingale, "Conscience Formation," 59.

Part II

1. Andrew Gelman, Jeffrey Fagan, and Alex Kiss, "An Analysis of the New York City Police Department's 'Stop-and-Frisk' Policy in the Context of Claims of Racial Bias," *Journal of the American Statistical Association* 102, no. 479 (2007): 816, 821–22; see again Bryan N. Massingale, "Conscience Formation and the Challenge of Unconscious Racial Bias," in *Conscience and Catholicism: Rights, Responsibilities, and Institutional Responses*, ed. David E. DeCosse and Kristin E. Heyer (Maryknoll, NY: Orbis Books, 2015), esp. 56–61.

Chapter 3

1. Congregation for the Doctrine of the Faith, "Instruction on Certain Aspects of the 'Theology of Liberation,'" August 6, 1984, IV.15, https://www .vatican.va/roman_curia/congregations/cfaith/documents/rc_con_cfaith _doc_19840806_theology-liberation_en.html; Congregation for the Doctrine of the Faith, "Instruction on Christian Freedom and Liberation," March 22, 1986, no. 74, https://www.vatican.va/roman_curia/congregations/cfaith /documents/rc_con_cfaith_doc_19860322_freedom-liberation_en.html.

2. Pope John Paul II, *Sollicitudo Rei Socialis* (Rome: Libreria Editrice Vaticana, 1987).

3. Conferencia General del Episcopado Latinoamericano (CELAM), "Justice," in *The Church in the Present-Day Transformation of Latin America in the Light of the Council: Second General Conference of Latin American Bishops, Bogotá, 24 August, Medellín, 26 August–6 September, Colombia, 1968,*

ed. Louis Michael Colonnese (Bogotá: General Secretariat of CELAM, 1973), 33. An online version of the bishops' text is available at http://people.loyno .edu/~quigley/Class/classjusticepeace.pdf.

4. Pope John Paul II, *Evangelium Vitae* (Rome: Libreria Editrice Vaticana, 1995).

5. Daniel K. Finn, "What Is a Sinful Social Structure?," *Theological Studies* 77, no. 1 (March 2016): 151.

6. *Catechism of the Catholic Church*, 2nd ed. (United States Catholic Conference—Libreria Editrice Vaticana, 1997).

7. Kevin Ahern, *Structures of Grace: Catholic Organizations Serving the Global Common Good* (Maryknoll, NY: Orbis Books, 2015), esp. 130–36.

8. Kenneth R. Himes, "Social Sin and the Role of the Individual," *Annual of the Society of Christian Ethics* 6 (1986): 213.

9. Pope John Paul II, *Veritatis Splendor* (Rome: Libreria Editrice Vaticana, 1993).

Chapter 4

1. Philip G. Zimbardo, "The Stanford Prison Experiment: A Simulation Study on the Psychology of Imprisonment," *Stanford Prison Experiment*, https://www.prisonexp.org.

2. Craig Haney, Curtis Banks, and Philip Zimbardo, "Interpersonal Dynamics in a Simulated Prison," *International Journal of Criminology and Penology* 1 (1973): 81.

3. Greene recounts a lot of this research in a popular book: Joshua D. Greene, *Moral Tribes: Emotion, Reason, and the Gap between Us and Them* (New York: Penguin Books, 2013).

4. Haidt presents this analysis and more in Jonathan Haidt, *The Righteous Mind: Why Good People Are Divided by Politics and Religion* (New York: Random House, 2012).

5. Conor M. Kelly, "The Nature and Operation of Structural Sin: Additional Insights from Theology and Moral Psychology," *Theological Studies* 80, no. 2 (June 2019): 301. The article also discusses the research of Greene and Haidt and its connection to structural sin in more detail.

6. See again Bryan N. Massingale, "Conscience Formation and the Challenge of Unconscious Racial Bias," in *Conscience and Catholicism: Rights, Responsibilities, and Institutional Responses*, ed. David E. DeCosse and Kristin E. Heyer (Maryknoll, NY: Orbis Books, 2015), esp. 56–61. See also Bryan

N. Massingale, *Racial Justice and the Catholic Church* (Maryknoll, NY: Orbis Books, 2010), 24–33.

Chapter 5

1. Lynne Peeples, "What the Data Say about Police Brutality and Racial Bias—and Which Reforms Might Work," *Nature*, May 26, 2021, https://www.nature.com/articles/d41586-020-01846-z.

2. Phillip Atiba Goff et al., *The Science of Justice: Race, Arrests, and Police Use of Force* (Los Angeles: Center for Policing Equity, 2016), https://policingequity.org/images/pdfs-doc/CPE_SoJ_Race-Arrests-UoF_2016-07-08-1130.pdf.

3. *Graham v. Connor*, 490 U.S., 386.

4. *Graham v. Connor*, 397.

5. Laurie Cassidy, "The Myth of the Dangerous Black Man," in *The Scandal of White Complicity in US Hyper-Incarceration: A Nonviolent Spirituality of White Resistance*, ed. Alex Mikulich, Laurie Cassidy, and Margaret Pfeil (New York: Palgrave Macmillan, 2013), 99, emphasis in original; see also 103–5.

6. Cassidy, "Myth of Dangerous Black Man," 90.

7. Stephen Menendian, "U.S. Neighborhoods Are More Segregated than a Generation Ago, Perpetuating Racial Inequity," *NBC News*, August 16, 2021, https://www.nbcnews.com/think/opinion/u-s-neighborhoods-are-more-segregated-generation-ago-perpetuating-racial-ncna1276372.

8. Calculations based on median net worth data from Neil Bhutta et al., "Disparities in Wealth by Race and Ethnicity in the 2019 Survey of Consumer Finances," *FEDS Notes*, September 28, 2020, https://www.federalreserve.gov/econres/notes/feds-notes/disparities-in-wealth-by-race-and-ethnicity-in-the-2019-survey-of-consumer-finances-20200928.htm.

9. For more on both the history of redlining and the present-day illustrations of housing discrimination (including the impact of zoning), see Richard Rothstein, *The Color of Law: A Forgotten History of How Our Government Segregated America* (New York: Liveright, 2017).

Chapter 6

1. Evaluation of data for May 16, 2020. Latoya Hill and Samathan Artiga, "COVID-19 Cases and Deaths by Race/Ethnicity: Current Data and Over Time," *KFF*, February 22, 2022, https://www.kff.org/coronavirus-covid-19

/issue-brief/covid-19-cases-and-deaths-by-race-ethnicity-current-data-and-changes-over-time/.

2. "Census Bureau Releases New Educational Attainment Data," *United States Census Bureau*, February 24, 2022, https://www.census.gov/newsroom/press-releases/2022/educational-attainment.html.

3. Sanne Magnan, "Social Determinants of Health 101 for Health Care: Five Plus Five," *National Academy of Medicine*, October 9, 2017, https://nam.edu/social-determinants-of-health-101-for-health-care-five-plus-five/.

4. Andrew Deener, "The Origins of the Food Desert: Urban Inequality as Infrastructural Exclusion," *Social Forces* 95, no. 3 (March 2017): 1285; see also 1291–98.

5. Jane W. Seymour et al., "The Role of Community Health Centers in Reducing Racial Disparities in Access to Primary Care," *Journal of Primary Care and Community Health* 8, no. 3 (2017): 147.

6. For these and other statistics on disparate health outcomes, see David C. Radley et al., "Achieving Racial and Ethnic Equity in U.S. Health Care: A Scorecard of State Performance," *The Commonwealth Fund*, November 11, 2021, https://www.commonwealthfund.org/publications/scorecard/2021/nov/achieving-racial-ethnic-equity-us-health-care-state-performance.

7. Ruqaijah Yearby, Brietta Clark, and José Figueroa, "Structural Racism in Historical and Modern US Health Care Policy," *Health Affairs* 41, no. 2 (2022): 189.

8. Michael T. Nietzel, "New Study: College Degree Carries Big Earnings Premium, but Other Factors Matter Too," *Forbes*, October 11, 2021, https://www.forbes.com/sites/michaeltnietzel/2021/10/11/new-study-college-degree-carries-big-earnings-premium-but-other-factors-matter-too/.

9. Allie Bidwell, "Wealthier Schools Send More Students to College," *U.S. News and World Report*, October 14, 2014, https://www.usnews.com/news/blogs/data-mine/2014/10/14/poverty-a-strong-predictor-of-college-enrollment.

10. Rachel Gable, quoted in Scott Jaschik, "The Hidden Curriculum," *Inside Higher Ed*, January 19, 2021, https://www.insidehighered.com/news/2021/01/19/author-discusses-her-new-book-first-generation-students-harvard-and-georgetown.

11. Jaschik, "Hidden Curriculum."

Part IV

1. Dorothy Day, "A Revolution Near Our Shores," *Selected Writings: By Little and By Little*, ed. Robert Ellsberg (Maryknoll, NY: Orbis Books, 1992), 303.

Chapter 7

1. "Seven Themes of Catholic Social Teaching," United States Conference of Catholic Bishops, https://www.usccb.org/beliefs-and-teachings/what-we -believe/catholic-social-teaching/seven-themes-of-catholic-social-teaching.

2. Kelly Johnson, "Catholic Social Teaching," in *Gathered for the Journey: Moral Theology in Catholic Perspective*, ed. David Matzko McCarthy and M. Therese Lysaught (Grand Rapids, MI: Eerdmans, 2007), 227.

3. Johnson, "Catholic Social Teaching," 227.

4. United States Conference of Catholic Bishops, *Economic Justice for All: Pastoral Letter on Catholic Social Teaching and the U.S. Economy* (Washington, DC: National Conference of Catholic Bishops, 1987), https://www.usccb .org/upload/economic_justice_for_all.pdf.

5. Timothy Dolan et al., "Letter to Congress on Moral Principles for Consideration for Health Care Reform and the Affordable Care Act," United States Conference of Catholic Bishops, March 8, 2017, https://www.usccb .org/resources/letter-congress-moral-principles-consideration-health-care -reform-and-affordable-care-act.

Chapter 8

1. Pope Benedict XVI, *Caritas in Veritate* (Rome: Libreria Editrice Vaticana, 2009).

2. David Cloutier, "Wanting 'The Best' for 'Our Kids': Parenting and Privilege," in *Sex, Love, and Families: Catholic Perspectives*, ed. Jason King and Julie Hanlon Rubio (Collegeville, MN: Liturgical Press Academic, 2020), 264.

3. Cloutier, "Wanting 'The Best,' " 266; see also 262–63, 265.

4. Meghan Clark, "Subsidiarity Is a Two-Sided Coin," *Catholic Moral Theology*, March 8, 2012, https://catholicmoraltheology.com/subsidiarity-is-a -two-sided-coin/, emphasis in original.

5. Bryan N. Massingale, *Racial Justice and the Catholic Church* (Maryknoll, NY: Orbis, 2010), 120.

6. Massingale, *Racial Justice*, 116.

Conclusion

1. *The Usual Suspects*, directed by Bryan Singer, 1995.

2. Jamie T. Phelps, "Joy Came in the Morning Risking Death for Resurrection: Confronting the Evils of Social Sin and Socially Sinful Structures,"

in *A Troubling in My Soul: Womanist Perspectives on Evil and Suffering*, ed. Emilie M. Townes (Maryknoll, NY: Orbis, 1993), 56.

3. "The Romero Prayer," *Archbishop Romero Trust*, http://www.romerotrust .org.uk/romero-prayer.

Recommended Resources for Further Theological Reflection

In keeping with the hope expressed in the conclusion that this book will be just the beginning of an ongoing journey, I want to provide a few suggested works that readers can use for their next steps. The list is, naturally, not exhaustive but will nonetheless provide starting points for the process of countering the injustice of racism with the eyes of faith. Indeed, many of these books have excellent bibliographies, so they can easily become stepping-stones to new sources that will help readers continue their journey.

Resources for Examining Racism Generally

Bryan N. Massingale, *Racial Justice and the Catholic Church* (Maryknoll, NY: Orbis, 2010).

Now *the* classic text offering a Catholic theological critique of racism in the United States (and the U.S. Catholic Church), Massingale's book develops the distinction between "commonsense racism" and the more encompassing "cultural form of racism" discussed in chapter 2 of this book. It also explores how Catholic theology can build a more robust response to both. Massingale's work is the place to begin for those looking to explore an even more robustly theological counter to the injustice of racism.

Edward K. Braxton, *The Church and the Racial Divide: Reflections of an African American Catholic Bishop* (Maryknoll, NY: Orbis, 2021).

Bishop Braxton's book collects a series of statements and pastoral letters about racism and the Black Catholic experience delivered during his years of active ministry. Eschewing many of the terms that are popular in secular discourse about racism in favor of a strictly theological reflection, Braxton's book represents a thoughtful opening that will be particularly useful for those who are hesitant to explore the issue of racism. Braxton's book is best read alongside Massingale's work, as the two represent a spectrum of approaches to racism in Catholic theology.

United States Conference of Catholic Bishops, *Open Wide Our Hearts: The Enduring Call to Love; A Pastoral Letter against Racism* (Washington, DC: United States Conference of Catholic Bishops, 2018), available online at https://www.usccb.org /resources/open-wide-our-hearts_0.pdf.

Regularly referenced throughout this book, the U.S. Catholic bishops' most recent pastoral letter on racism is worth reading in its entirety for the way it speaks to the realities of racism in the United States today—at both the personal and the social level—and the way it articulates the need for a heartier Catholic response.

Daniel P. Horan, O.F.M., *A White Catholic's Guide to Racism and Privilege* (Notre Dame, IN: Ave Maria Press, 2021).

For those looking to explore more of the categories used in contemporary discourse around racism—things like privilege, white supremacy, and the social construction of "whiteness"— Horan's book provides a detailed introduction. The focus is primarily on helping Catholics understand and contextualize the common secular language, so Horan's book will be most useful for those who feel they have a comfortable grasp with the theological rationale for confronting racism as a sin.

Resources for Fostering the Practical Work of Conversion

Patrick Saint-Jean, S.J., *The Spiritual Work of Racial Justice: A Month of Meditations with Ignatius of Loyola* (Vestal, NY: Anamchara Books, 2021).
A beautiful set of guided reflections modeled on the themes found in St. Ignatius of Loyola's *Spiritual Exercises* (sin, Christology, the passion and death, resurrection and new life), Saint-Jean's text outlines a step-by-step process for the spiritual work of conversion described in chapter 1 of this book. This book is an excellent tool for getting a better sense of where racism intersects with our interior lives and identifying ways we can still be transformed.

Christopher Pramuk, *Hope Sings, So Beautiful: Graced Encounters across the Color Line* (Collegeville, MN: Liturgical Press, 2013). Through reflections on the stories, voices, and artistic representations of a diverse array of thinkers who have fought for hope in their lives, Pramuk provides a detailed, and deeply personal, account of his own ongoing conversion process, yielding a practical spirituality for readers willing to meet his vulnerability with their own.

Ignatian Solidarity Network, *A Parish Journey for Racial Justice and Equity*, available online at https://ignatiansolidarity.net /resources/faith-in-action-responding-to-racial-injustice/#tab -id-8.
Although the resources are aimed primarily at Jesuit parishes, the videos, workbooks, and PowerPoints available through this Ignatian Solidarity Network program can serve as the basis for parish-wide efforts to respond to racism in the United States.